Ivories
in the Collection of the Seattle Art Museum

Gail Joice,
Michael Knight,
and Pamela McClusky

This publication has been generously supported by a grant from the National Endowment for the Arts.

© 1987 Seattle Art Museum
All rights reserved

Printed in Japan
ISBN 0-932216-25-0
LC 87-061753
Designed by Corinna Campbell
Photography by Paul Macapia

cover: Covered open-worked box; Chinese, Qing dynasty; ivory; Eugene Fuller Memorial Collection, 35.282

Unless otherwise noted, all objects illustrated in this catalogue are ivory.

Foreword

The subject of this publication is ivory carving, and although the objects presented are all fine examples of the versatility of the medium and the skill of its carvers, for me the real interest here lies in the differences in the ways various cultures used and regarded this treasured material. The Seattle Art Museum is fortunate to have a varied and rich collection from which to draw ivory carvings representing many cultures—the ancient Mediterranean, medieval Europe, India, Japan, China, and many African cultures. We are also fortunate to have on our staff the three individuals who contributed their scholarship and spirit of collaboration to make this project possible.

Gail Joice, Registrar and Head of Museum Services, selected four objects from our classical and European collections. All of these objects were gifts to the museum, two from the Fullers, the founding family. Again drawing on the magnificent legacy left the museum by the Fuller's, Michael Knight, Assistant Curator in the Asian Art Department, describes four Chinese objects, four Indian carvings, one dating from as long ago as the fifth century, and a group of four Japanese netsuke. Pamela McClusky, Curator of the Art of Africa, Oceania, and the Americas, presents seven objects, some of which are purely African in origin and several of which undoubtedly speak of European influences.

It is hoped that this small selection from the museum's holdings and the discussion provided will lead the reader across three continents to explore the fascinating story of ivory in terms of its cultural and artistic background. As a result of this publication, ivory carvings from around the world and their significance as a form of artistic expression will no doubt become more meaningful to the interested reader and museum visitor in search of knowledge.

Henry Trubner
Associate Director
Art and the Collections

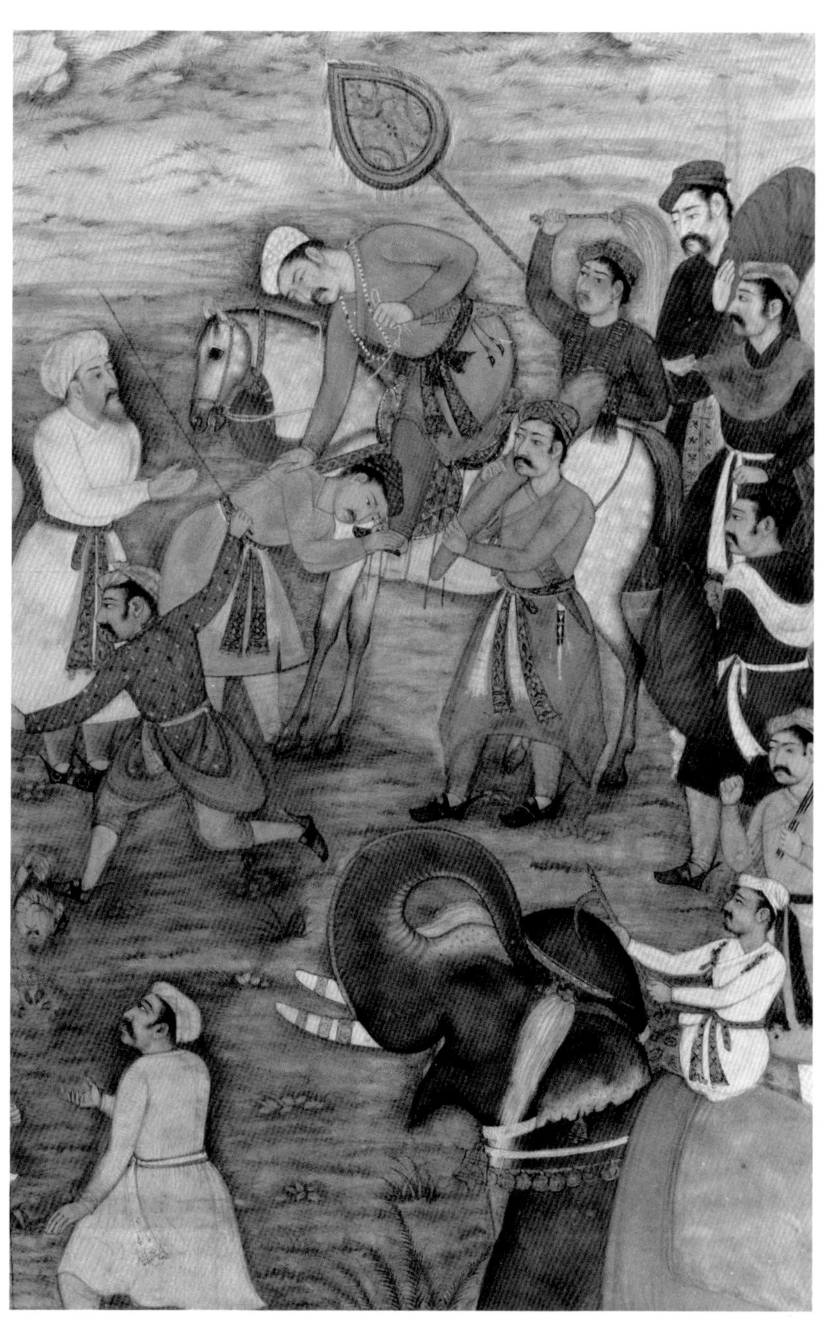

Akbar on Horseback receiving Homage (detail);
Indian, Mughal dynasty, reign of Akbar, 1556-1605
colors and gold on paper; H: 9 ¾″, W: 5 ¾″;
Eugene Fuller Memorial Collection, 41.204

Introduction

Ivory is a distinctive medium. It is tempting to touch, with a luminous smooth surface well suited for objects that are handled constantly—bracelets, combs, buttons, utensils, ritual objects, and holders of all sorts. It absorbs colors and oils to take on a large tonal range of patinas from a bleached white to a warm blond or a deep mahogany. It has unique properties for an artist to consider. The minute tubular structure of elephant tusks, from which most ivory derives, results in a uniformly fine grain, which allows ivory to hold intricate detail, and the material is easily carved with woodworking tools. The curve and size of the tusk define strict limitations and offer particular challenges. Many carvers have taken advantage of these qualities to create ivory compositions of exquisite detail and rich texture.

However, some of the qualities that give ivory its unique character are also responsible for the relative scarcity of early examples. Like many organic materials, ivory is susceptible to a certain degree of rot. It is also sensitive to changes in environment; the layers created as the tusk grows and which give ivory some of its luminescent beauty will separate and crack if exposed to rapid changes in temperature and humidity. Although it is a relatively strong material, ivory is prone to breakage, particularly when it has aged and weakened. It is for these reasons that few early ivories have survived, even from countries like India where the material was relatively common.

Nevertheless, there is archaeological evidence that ivory was employed as an artists' material since Paleolithic times when carvers inscribed designs on pieces of mammoth tusk in French caves some 40,000 years ago. One of the world's oldest art media, ivory has been used and appreciated by a wide range of peoples, from the earliest times to the present. However, not all cultures uniformly value ivory as a choice for artistic efforts. In Asia, Europe, and Africa, ivory is surrounded with divergent associations and meanings.

Asia

China

The Chinese have a propensity to assign particular virtues to plants, animals, and other materials, for instance the pine, plum, and bamboo are known as the "three friends of winter," and have associated with them certain desirable human characteristics such as resiliance and loyalty. In part due to such associations, these materials are popular in art both as motifs and media; many are mentioned in art and ritual texts from the Zhou dynasty (mid-11th century-221 B.C.). Although the Chinese began to carve ivory and bone in the Neolithic period (the earliest find so far is from the Hemudu site in Zhejiang province and dates to around 5,000 B.C.), it has none of these virtuous associations and is rarely mentioned in texts. Even in more recent times, when Chinese carved ivories were popular in the trade with the West, this material was rarely mentioned in Chinese art or trade manifestos.

The Chinese elite seems to have felt that objects made from ivory were best described by the term *su*, which roughly translates as vulgar. This was a term the Chinese literati used to describe arts that were not in their refined taste; it was applied to certain types of decorative paintings, lacquers, textiles, and other overly elaborate or ostentatious arts and crafts. Thus ivory was sought after for its decorative uses, not its virtuous associations, and the production and exchange of ivory carvings is difficult to document in China. Certainly the majority of carved figurines was made for religious use either in the home or in temples. Functional objects such as brush rests, brush holders, and seals were probably intended for the wealthy merchant class, scholar-officials, and for use in court. In addition, many objects were made for export.

The identities of the craftsmen who carved ivory is also hard to trace. Ivory carvers are mentioned in the imperial records, particularly during the Qing dynasty (1644-1911), but the actual carvers seem to have spent only short times at the capital and had their main places of work elsewhere. It is unlikely that many craftsmen specialized in carving ivory; rather, it is most likely that carvers of wood, rhinocerous horn, and other similar materials also worked in ivory.

The major known ivory carving locations were near export centers where this material was readily available and incidentally where outside influences were most deeply felt. The sources of this valuable and rare commodity for most extant Chinese carvings were Southeast Asia and, later, Africa. A species of the Asian elephant did live in China apparently in some numbers in the Bronze Age and early imperial China. These creatures became increasingly scarce as China's population grew; they were uncommon by the Tang dynasty (618-906) and almost unknown outside of the imperial zoos and the deep south by the Ming (1368-1644).

India

The ivory available in India came from several sources. Though now in danger of extinction, elephants are native to India. Tusks are limited to the male of the Indian elephant and are not as large as those found on the African elephant. The elephant with tusks served as an important beast of burden and a symbol of power in India, and relatively few would have been sacrificed for their ivory. So while some of the many ivories carved in India were from Indian elephants, much of the ivory for later Indian carving, and virtually all of the larger pieces, must have been imported from Africa.

There were several centers of ivory production in India, including Delhi, Murshidabad, Mysore, and Travancore. An important later center developed in Orissa. While ivory, even African ivory, did not have the scale to be used for individual sculptures in large Buddhist, Hindu, or Jain temples, it played a role of some importance in smaller religious sculpture, as inlay in larger pieces, and in the decorative arts.

The carving of ivory to create sculpture and decorative materials has a long history in India, and although few early examples have survived, the importance of this tradition can be traced in religious texts and through descriptions recorded in Indian literary sources and in those of other nationalities. As early as the fifth century B.C., ivory played a significant role in trade between India and other nations: examples of Indian ivory carving have been found at Pompeii and at Begram in Afghanistan and are discussed in Roman texts.

Japan

Unlike either China or India, Japan does not have an ancient tradition of ivory carving. The elephant is not native to Japan, and ivory was always a rare medium. Although ivory did have several uses in Japan, including small sculpture, inlays, and decoration, by far the most frequent and best-known ivory carvings are the small toggles known as netsuke. These sculptures were carved from small pieces of ivory, often material left over from other uses. Recognizing the value of his medium, the Japanese netsuke carver often shaped his object to fit the profiles of the ivory he was provided and took full advantage of the color and ease of carving of the material to create surprisingly successful small-scale sculpture. Netsuke frequently represent human figures or animals and are amazingly naturalistic, owing both to the carvers' skill and the material in which they worked.

Western World

Ivory was prized in the Western world as a precious material; its creamy color and the beauty of its polished surface gave it a gemlike status. It was frequently set into precious metals, from early chryselephantine (gold and ivory) statues of classical Greece to Christian manuscript covers for the European medieval church.

Ancient Mediterranean

Ivory carving was a pervasive tradition in the ancient Mediterranean world and dates from the time of predynastic Egypt (before 3100 B.C.). Elephant ivory from Nubia and Syria supplied the needs of the master craftsmen under the pharaohs for objects such as small-scale portrait sculpture, seals, utensils, toilette articles, and decorative inlay. The Phoenicians transported African and Syrian ivory by sea route within the Mediterranean and might have brought Indian ivory to the area as well.

The Bronze Age civilization of the Aegean supported a great outpouring of ivory carving, in both Minoan Crete and Mycenaean Greece. A wealth of ivory carvings was found in the treasury of the Palace of Knossos, sealed by an earthquake in 1570 B.C. Hoards of elephant tusks that had been imported from Syria in raw form were found in the ruins of other Minoan palaces that were destroyed by a volcanic cataclysm circa 1450 B.C. There are many references to the decorative use of ivory in Homer's *Odyssey,* including descriptions of it in King Menelaus's palace at Sparta.

Ivory carving reached a high point of technical and artistic excellence in Greece of the fifth century B.C., with the colossal chryselephantine statues by Phidias at Athens and Olympia, famous throughout the Greek empire.

Medieval Europe

In medieval Europe, ivory carried important historical and biblical associations which enhanced the appreciation of its physical beauty. Some ivories were regarded as having magical properties and some were reputed to be the mythical horn of a unicorn—the fantastic beast that was a symbol of Christ in the medieval bestiary. In religious objects, ivory was associated with functions of purity. It also served as an emblem of power in the secular customs of royalty.

Throughout European history, ivory has been sought after for both religious and secular carvings, which were commissioned or purchased by wealthy patrons. Some of the most noted examples were created at the artistic center of Paris which began to draw ivory craftsmen from monastery workshops beginning in the eleventh century. The rise of the Gothic cathedrals in the late twelfth century opened a rich market for religious ivories used in the decoration of private chapels for the nobility. By the fourteenth century affluent patrons commissioned secular ivory objects such as luxuriously carved combs, mirror cases, and jewel caskets. These prized possessions of the Gothic noblewoman carried secular themes of decoration based on a new genre, that of chivalric love.

In the seventeenth and eighteenth centuries, with a regular supply of ivory from West Africa, the production of ivory carvings in Germany surpassed that of any other country in Europe at the time. The medium became a popular obsession and was used in great diversity, from small-scale sculpture and portrait medallions to tobacco graters and surgical instruments. German technical innovations, such as the use of a lathe for production of virtuoso turned pieces, led the field of ivory carving in Holland, Flanders, and England early in the seventeenth century.

Africa

Well before West Africa became a major emporium for the ivory trade, many African cultures regarded ivory as more than a profitable commodity. Burial sites of the past as well as practices of the present indicate that ivory was often a sign of high rank or status. Archaeological finds in various parts of Africa indicate that ivory was often buried with rulers and prestigious persons. This tendency can be traced back in the Igbo culture to the tenth century. A burial chamber at Igbo-Ukwu, Nigeria, excavated in the 1960s revealed a dignitary seated in opulent dress with one foot resting on top of a large elephant tusk. Today, Igbo individuals with title still equate their wealth with the action of "taking the horn" or acquiring a tusk as a prerogative of leadership.

European enthusiasm for ivory doubtless reinforced notions of its monetary value and many African rulers became adept at stockpiling ivories to keep control over the vast trading networks that emerged. Such monopolies enhanced the value of ivory as a treasured gift, bride price, and tribute in certain cultures.

Ivory's cost and rarity may not have contributed to its elevated associations in West Africa nearly so much as its animal of origin. Elephants are a prevalent leadership symbol in a continent where they once roamed wild, never to be domesticated and to be hunted with risk. Their tusks, which grow to six to ten feet in length, became an emblem of the ponderous animal whose stamina and strength are readily admired. Among the Yoruba of Nigeria, a chant about elephants sung by hunters expresses respect for their formidable power:

> Elephant who brings death. Elephant, a spirit in the bush.
> With his single hand he can pull two palm trees to the ground.
> If he had two hands—
> He would tear the heavens like an old rag.
> With his four mortar legs—he tramples down the grass.
> Wherever he walks, the grass is forbidden to stand up again.
> An elephant is not a load for an old man—
> Nor for a young man either.
>
> (Gbadamosi and Beier, 1959, p. 34)

Africa has supplied the world with ivory since at least the second millenium B.C. Ancient Egypt was furnished with ivory by Nubians who hunted elephants in the vicinity of Meroe and Ed Debba. During the era of Roman North Africa, elephants were sought not only for ivory but for the Roman circus games. By the fourth century A.D., North African elephants had been hunted to extinction, and trans-Saharan traders took over this lucrative market. Caravans carried tusks from West Africa through the oasis trade routes to satisfy the Mediterranean demand for ivory. Tusks were also traded on the East African coast to Indian Ocean merchants from the Greco-Roman, Arab, Persian, and Asian worlds.

Europe was required to go through these costly channels until the "Age of Discovery" in the fifteenth century, when navigators sailed down the Atlantic coast and found vast quantities of ivory at very little cost. Portuguese records reveal that "an ivory spoon cost less than two quires of paper, an ivory salt cellar less than a linen shirt" (Ryder, 1964). In 1514, more than 10,000 pounds of ivory were auctioned off in Lisbon alone. An intense and competitive trade in ivory was established on the West Coast and continued until the herds of elephants that roamed large stretches of West Africa were depleted at the turn of this century.

To supply the fast-growing markets for ivory in Asia, Europe, and America in the nineteenth century, ivory traders turned to East and Central Africa as sources. It is estimated that over 50,000 elephants were killed annually during the last half of the century. In 1900, perhaps stirred on by the decline of the buffalo herds in North America, an international conference was convened to declare sanctuaries for elephants (an idea that was not implemented in many parts of Africa until the 1970s). Today, there is a total ban on private trade in wildlife trophies, skins, and ivory in many African countries. An international committee issues licenses for importation of ivory, now with a market value of nearly $40,000 per tusk. Dismaying documentation of the drastic decline of the population of this awesome mammal is finally becoming a worldwide concern.

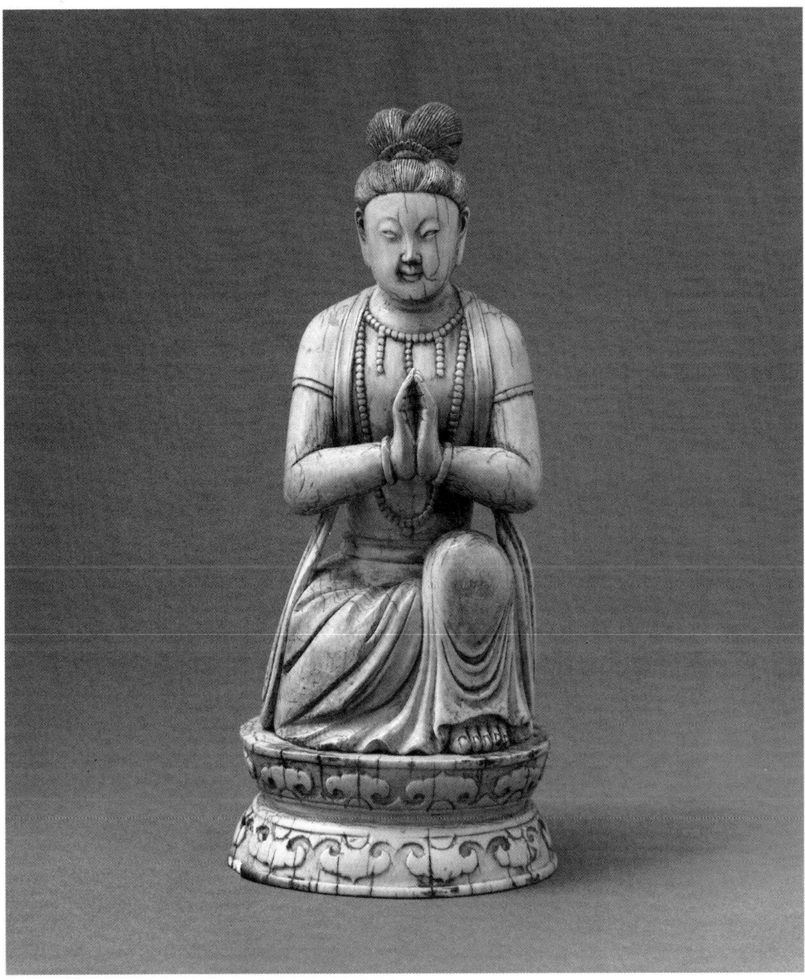

China

1. *Guanyin*
Chinese, Ming dynasty, 16th-17th century
H: 8⅛″
Eugene Fuller Memorial Collection, 66.7

The most extensive use of ivory in China from the Neolithic period through the middle of the Ming dynasty (1368-1644) was for decorative and functional items such as vessels, hair pins, certain types of musical instruments, and inlays into other materials. Ivory sculpture was relatively rare and very little has survived to the present. At the beginning of the sixteenth century this situation was beginning to change, and by late in the century, the carving of figures in ivory had become dominant in certain areas. This figure carving tradition developed along the Fujian coastline largely in response to contact with the West. The city most noted for ivory, as well as many other materials destined for the Western market, was the port of Zhangzhou. The arrival of Western traders provided two important conditions for the development of an ivory carving industry in this area: a ready source of the material and a market for the finished product. Religious figures were the items most frequently commissioned from the carvers in Zhangzhou, and the *guanyin* and child, who closely resemble the Virgin and Child, was the most common group portrayed in Chinese ivories of the late sixteenth century. The skills of the Zhangzhou carvers and merchants soon opened up markets for other ivory figures of both Western and purely Chinese origin, and the ivory carving industry flourished and spread to other areas.

The dating and provenance of this *guanyin* presents certain problems. Unlike the vast majority of the ivory carvings of *guanyin* created by the Zhangzhou carvers in the late sixteenth and seventeenth centuries, this figure relates closely to Buddhist sculpture of the Song (960-1279), Yuan (1260-1368), and Ming dynasty and reveals almost no evidence of Western influence. The bared chest, elaborate coiffure, string beads, and symbolic hand gesture (mudra) contrast with the usually fully clad and much more feminine and demure figures from Zhangzhou. Carved from a solid piece of ivory, this figure is shown kneeling in a relaxed and naturalistic pose on a double-lotus plinth. The naturalism carries through to details such as the toes and fingernails, and the fleshy, youthful face. On the basis of comparison with Buddhist figures in other media, this figure has tentatively been dated to the late sixteenth century.

2. Ceremonial tablet *(hu)*
Chinese, Ming-Qing dynasty, 17th-18th century
H: 18⅛″
Eugene Fuller Memorial Collection, 57.119

In China ivory does not appear in the major ritual texts and is rarely recorded in other literature. However, it was an important medium for at least one major ritual form: the ceremonial tablet *(hu)* that court officials carried when making an appearance before the emperor. Inscribed with the rank of the official, these long, flat plaques date from at least as early as the Tang dynasty (618-906). Ceramic burial figures of court officials from this period are frequently depicted carrying these tablets, which were held upright in front of the body in both hands. A flat section cut from an elephant tusk and retaining the curve of that tusk proved ideal for this purpose. Many ivory *hu* were made from the Tang to the Ming dynasty. Their official use was discontinued during the Qing dynasty (1644-1911), but *hu* continued to be made for the antiquarian market.

This piece has the standard flat curved shape of the *hu* and is deeply stained, indicating it has been handled frequently. The *hu* of the Ming dynasty was plain except for the insignia of the rank of the carrier; yet this tablet is elaborately decorated with incised figures in landscape, garden, and architectural settings. There is no insignia of rank. This may indicate an early Qing dynasty date. There are a number of men, women, and children incised onto both surfaces of this piece. All are elegantly dressed in Ming dynasty style and are shown at leisurely pursuits in various settings. They may portray scenes from one of the popular novels or plays of the seventeenth or early eighteenth century.

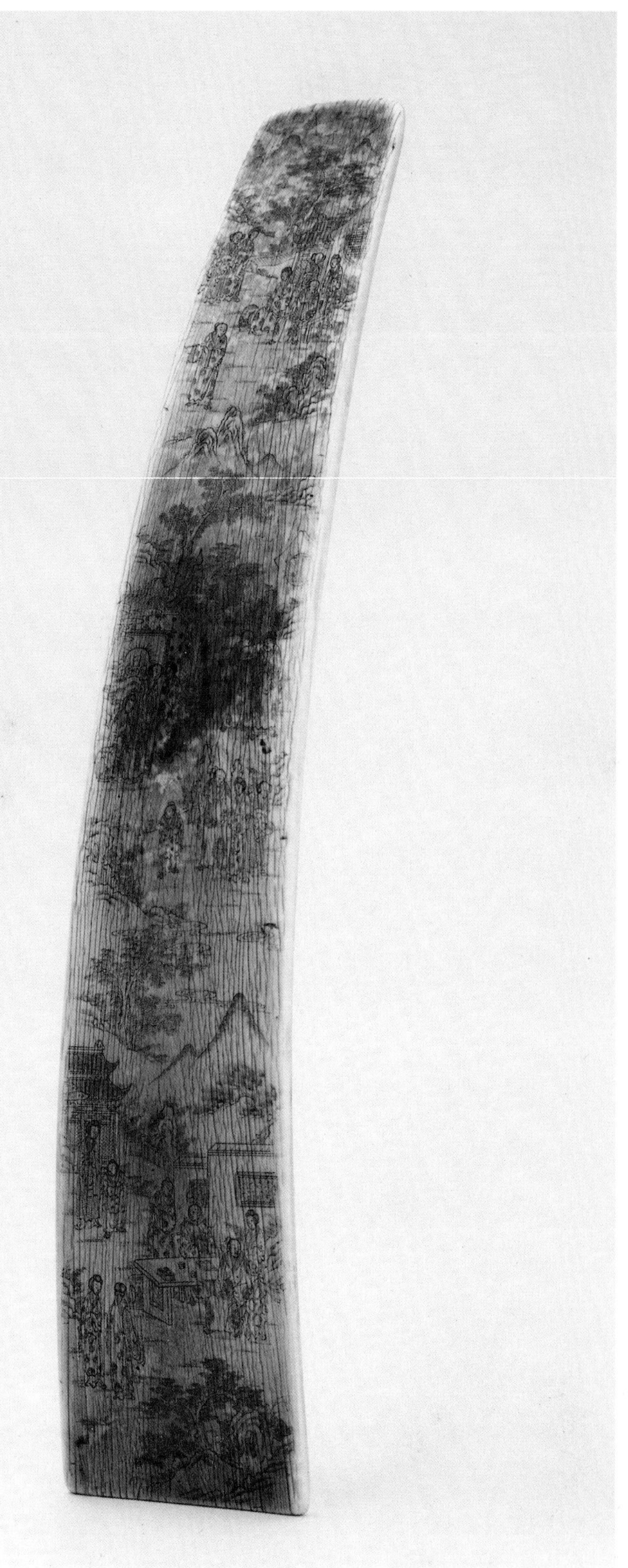

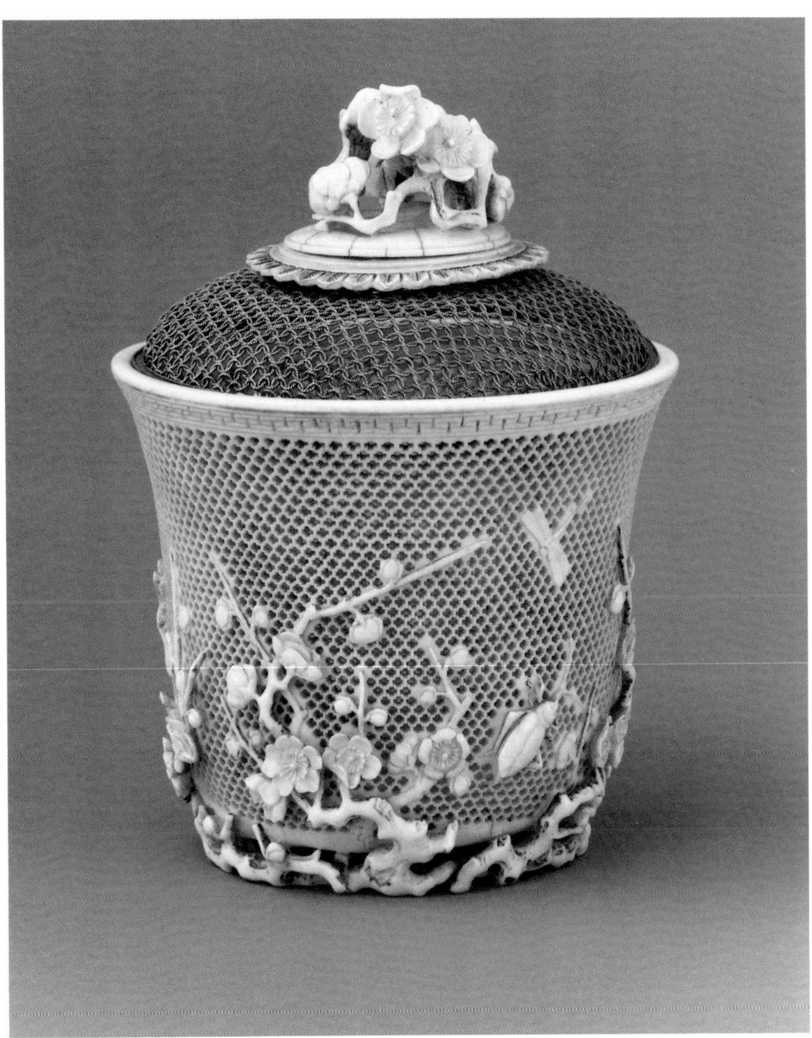

3. Covered open-worked box
Chinese, Qing dynasty, possibly reign of the Qianlong emperor (1736-95)
H: 5 ⅜″
Eugene Fuller Memorial Collection, 35.282

Because of its density, ivory can be carved very thin with a great number of openings and undercutting; the ease with which it can be worked allows fine detailing. As can be seen in this box, these qualities were fully explored by Chinese ivory carvers during the Qing dynasty. It is for exquisite open-worked boxes and fans created during the nineteenth and early twentieth centuries that Chinese ivory craftsmen are best known in the West.

This box is remarkable for having a large amount of openwork in combination with highly developed three-dimensional carving. The body of the box, which is actually quite thick, is given a thin, light appearance by the cross-shaped openings separated by only a slight border of ivory. The foot of the box is carved as a series of gnarled plum branches which continue part way up the side of the body where they are covered with blossoms. Around the base of the box, the trunks of the plum branches are carved fully in the round and the blossoms on the side are deeply undercut. Flying and crawling around the blossoms are four insects: a beetle, a dragonfly, a butterfly, and what appears to be a mosquito—all are finely carved with natural detail. A key fret border surrounds the top of the body, and the inside has been carved with a slight shelf which holds the cover.

The cover of the box consists of woven pairs of twisted wire supporting a piece of carved ivory. This piece of ivory also takes the form of flowering plum branches carved fully in the round; partially hidden under them is a sprig of bamboo. They rest on a circle of ivory which has a border of leaves. Open-worked boxes of this type were filled with flower petals and other fragrant materials. The openwork allowed the scent to escape into the surrounding room.

4. Wrist rest
Chinese, Qing dynasty, 18th-early 19th century
H: 9⅝″
Eugene Fuller Memorial Collection, 33.874

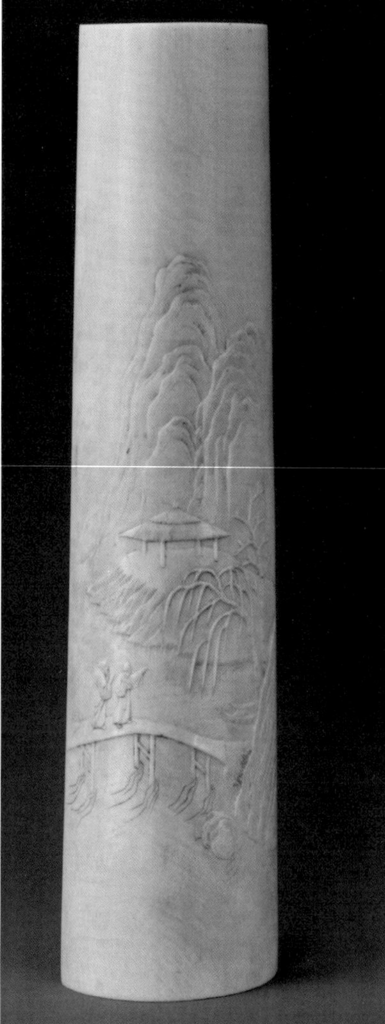

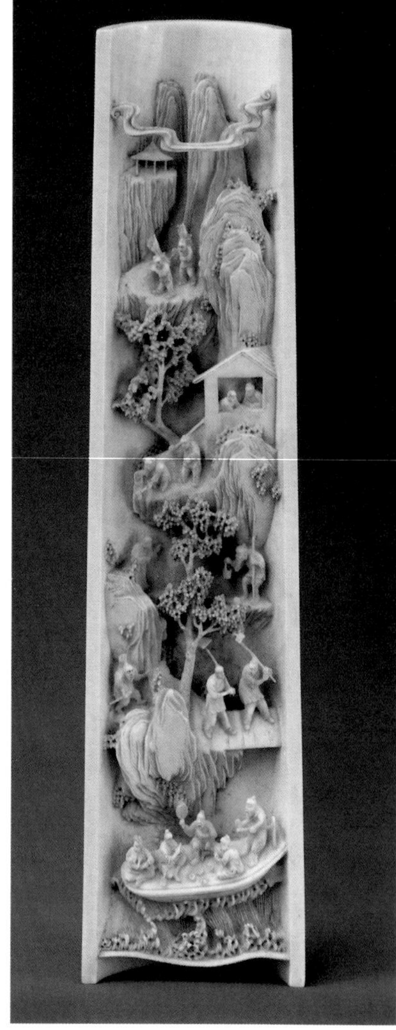

Particularly important in writing lengthy official documents with brush and ink, the Chinese wrist rest was a part of the paraphernalia found on the desk of the scholar-official. The form of the wrist rest and its decoration were in part determined by its function: it had to be high enough to keep the hand, arm, and any garments clear of the writing surface, it had to be long enough to be stable and comfortable, and the outer surface had to be smooth and of a shape to allow the arm to move freely. Because a half cylinder about one to two inches high and about eight to twelve inches long proved ideal, a split stem of a bamboo or a carved ivory tusk was the favored media for these objects. Because it is hollow, bamboo can only be carved on the outer surface; thus, as a medium for wrist rests, it has limited decorative potential. Ivory on the other hand, can be carved in great detail on its inner surface, a potential fully exploited in many wrist rests. The Chinese ivory carver frequently used both halves of a split tusk for a pair of wrist rests, carving each as the mirror image of the other. In this way, one half, carved in shallow relief, could be used as a wrist rest while the other half was displayed on the desk with the highly detailed interior carving exposed.

The themes depicted in the ivory wrist rest of the Qing dynasty are similar to those in other decorative arts of that period. Particularly popular were landscapes occupied by scholars, hermits, or farmers. Other favorites included Buddhist sages, immortals, and flowers, birds, and insects. The wrist rest illustrated here is a fine example of the landscape genre. Portrayed on the exterior of this piece are two scholars on a bridge enjoying their surroundings. Mountains, rocks, and even the current in the stream are clearly depicted despite the shallow relief carving. The interior of the piece is carved in high relief and portrays an idealized mountain scene. At the base of this mountain is a boat occupied by boatmen and gentlemen enjoying wine. Farther up are a pair of farmers with hoes, a wood gatherer, two gentlemen enjoying the view from a pavilion, peasants seeking water, and more wood gatherers. Near the top of the cloud-banded precipitous peak is another viewing pavilion. Farmers and wood gatherers often appear in Daoist and Chan Buddhist writings as hermits who have found the true way and have escaped the chaos of the day-to-day world. Combined with the gentlemen enjoying nature, this scene must have been especially delightful to the scholar-official as he toiled at his duties.

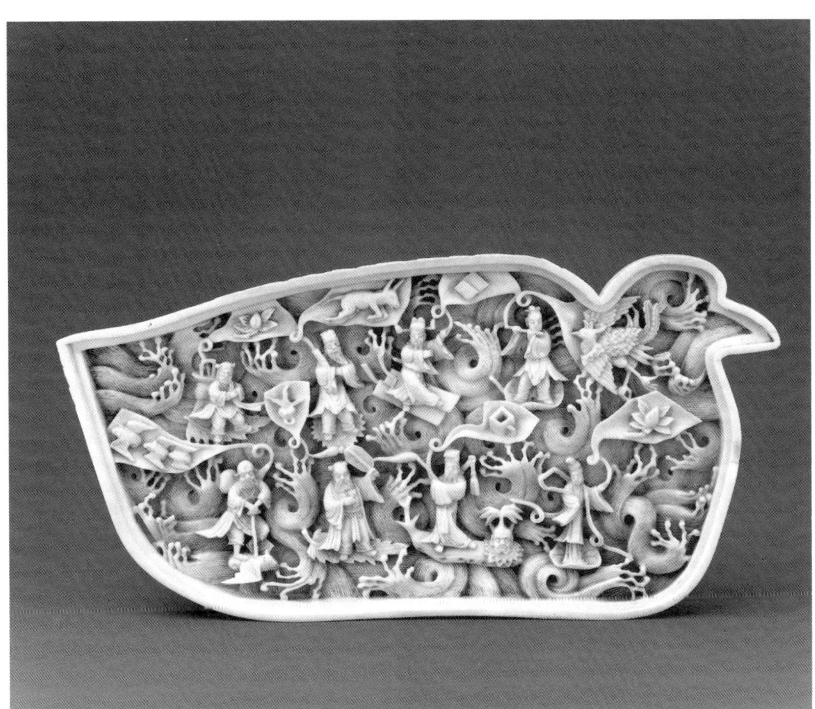

5. Gift box in the shape of a duck
Chinese, Qing dynasty, 18th-19th century
H: 3 7/8″; L: 7 3/4″
Eugene Fuller Memorial Collection, 54.60

This box offers an example of two of the qualities that the Chinese carver was able to exploit in ivory. The relative simplicity of the decor on the exterior of the box reveals the warm character of the surface of ivory and its ability to take a stain, while the elaborate interior displays the extent to which this material could be carved. The box is in the shape of a duck with a stiff outline and detailed but rather mechanical carving depicting the feathers. The majority of the carving is restricted to the wings, back, and tail which are further highlighted by staining with a black substance, most likely ink. The box is cut through the center with the sections mirror images of each other. In startling contrast to this restrained exterior, the interior of the box is heavily decorated with swirling, stylized waves, human figures, and numerous symbolic animals, plants, and objects.

The interiors of both halves of the box contain the same figures who can be identified as one version of the Eight Daoist Immortals according to various symbols and the pennants they hold. In the upper section near the head of the duck is Han Xiangxi with a flute and a phoenix on his pennant; to his right is Cao Guojiu, who wears official's robes, stands on his castanets, and holds a banner which bears a book. To his right is Zhang Guolao who carries a bamboo drum to which is attached a pennant with a white mule. Near the tail of the duck, Lan Caihe is shown carrying a basket on his back; a pennant bearing a flower is attached to the basket. Below him is Li Tieguai leaning on his staff and carrying a gourd and pennant decorated with three bats; to his left is Zhongli Chuan, a fat gentleman with a fan. Beside him is Lu Dongbin, who stands on a demon (which has the body of a whale and a demon's head) and carries a fly whisk and sword. His pennant, which is attached to the whisk, bears a cup. The only woman of the Eight Daoist Immortals, He Xiangu, stands on a leaf and is identified by the lotus blossom on her pennant. The figures and waves completely fill the box, which is only seven and one-half inches long. Considering the scale of the box, these figures show remarkable detail and the carver's control of the medium.

The purpose of this box is not entirely clear. The complexity of the iconography suggests that it was made for the Chinese market or at least for an area where these figures were known. Because the interior is so elaborately carved, it could have served no practical function, and most likely it was intended as an expensive gift. The style of the carving on this piece relates to carvings in jade, wood, and lacquer of the late Qing dynasty. Auspicious objects, literary themes, and legends such as the Eight Daoist Immortals were popular motifs in decorative arts of the late Qing.

India

6. Monkey

North Indian, Kushan-early Gupta period, 2nd-5th century
H: 7 ¼″
Eugene Fuller Memorial Collection, 51.58

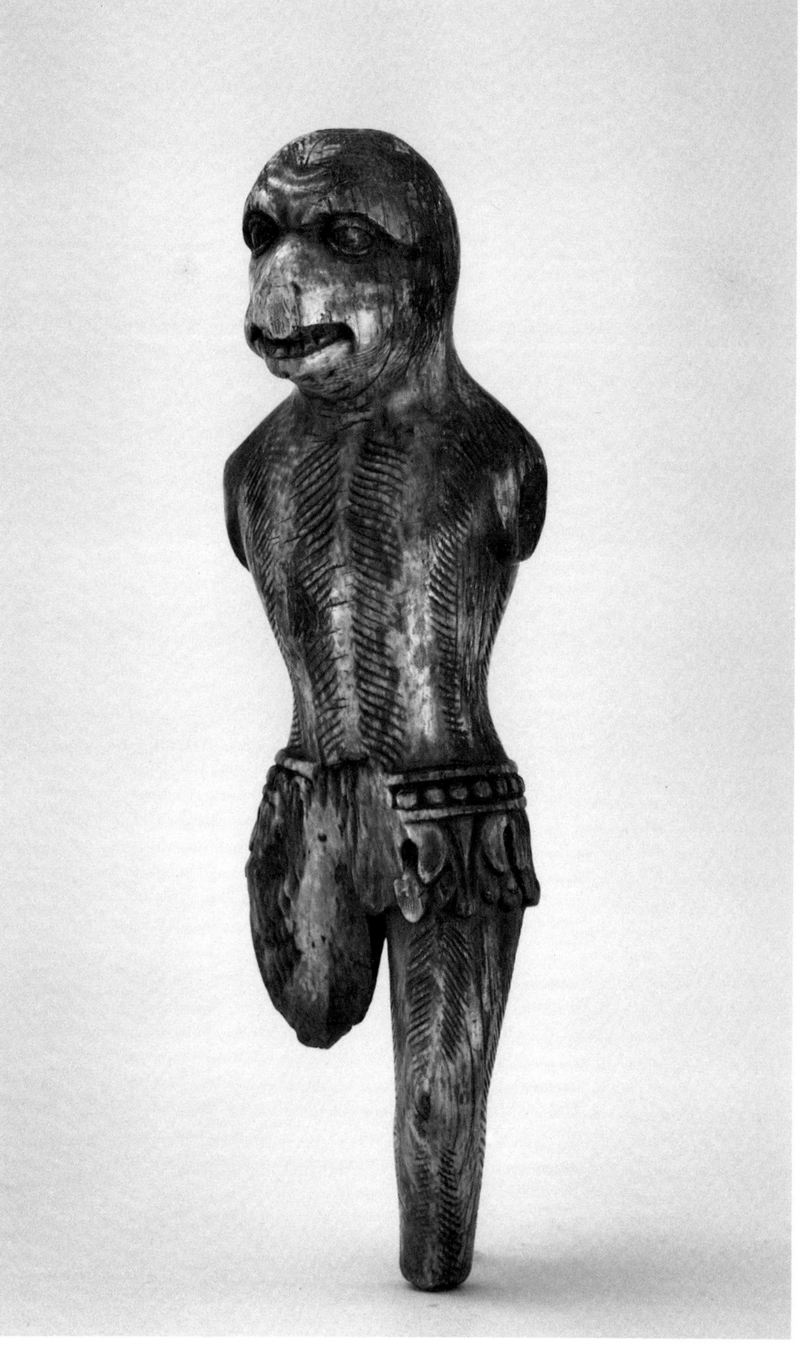

Northern India during the Kushan period and on into the early part of the Gupta was an area with diverse cultural influences. Buddhism was the prevalent religion and the majority of the extant arts are of Buddhist themes. However, sculptural styles were influenced by the remains of the Greco-Roman tradition, which had existed in this region from the time of the conquests of Alexander the Great, and had been maintained by trade and conquest across this area and on to China via the silk road. This monkey reveals such an influence in the linear incising which suggests fur, in the pseudo acanthus leaf girdle, and even in the treatment of the eyes.

The exact function of this sculpture and even its religious significance are unclear. In Buddhist art, the monkey appears most frequently in Jataka tales, stories about the various incarnations of the Buddha. As such, the monkey would logically appear as part of a larger group. However, the three-dimensional treatment and the scale of this figure seem to point away from this theme. The Hindu monkey god Hanuman appeared as a cult figure in the Gupta period, and it is possible that this is a very early representation of this deity. However, Hanuman was rarely shown in an ensemble with other figures. This piece is a striking example of the early use of ivory in relatively small-scale, three-dimensional sculpture, and as such offers clues to what may have been a much more extensive use of this medium.

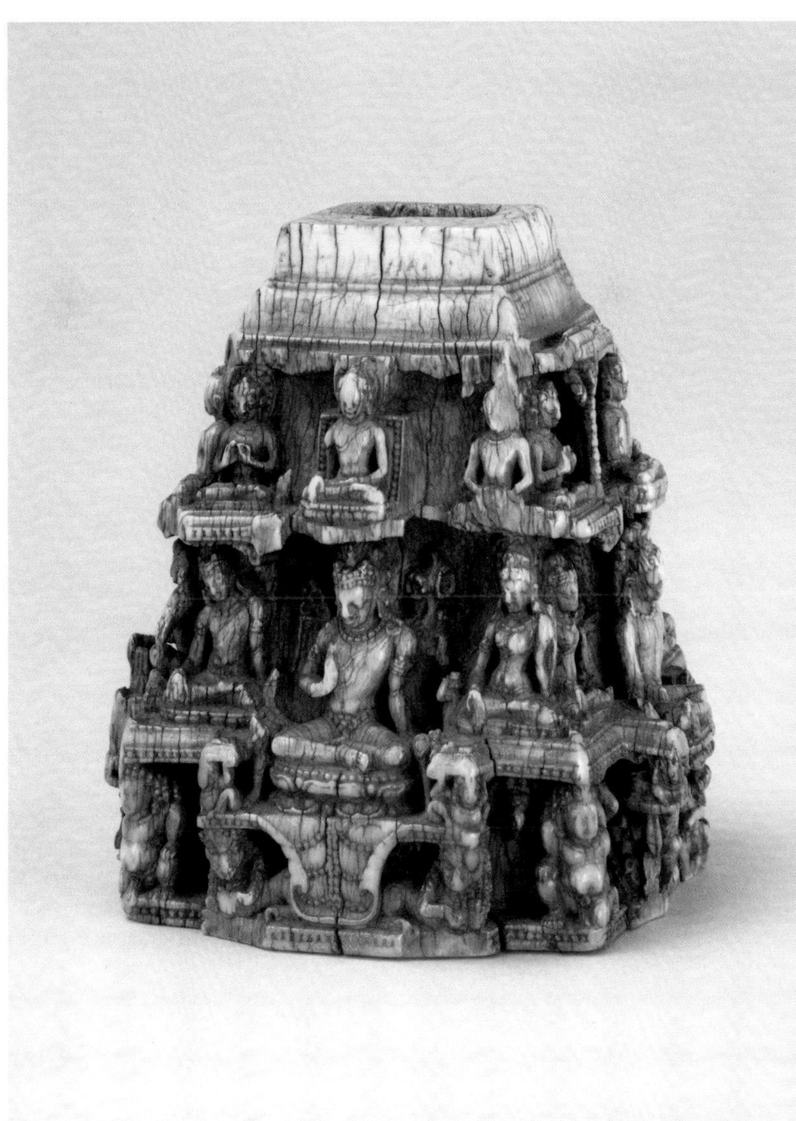

7. Stupa with Dhyana Buddhas, bodhisattvas, and attendants
Indian, from Bihar or Bengal, Pala period, 10th century
H: 4 ½ ″
Eugene Fuller Memorial Collection, 48.166

The Seattle Art Museum is fortunate to have two early examples of three-dimensional Indian sculpture in ivory: the monkey (no. 6) and this stupa, which reveals the complexity attained by the Indian craftsman working in ivory as early as the tenth century. Although only four-and-one-half inches in height, this piece is divided into three distinct layers, each carved with a multiplicity of figures and complex architectural detailing. The lowest level is the most complex. At each of the four corners is a nude dwarflike figure *(lokapala)* who supports the platform of the next layer. In the center of each side are additional figures that support the thrones of the bodhisattvas above them: these figures are lions to the north and south and monkeys and humans to the east and west. The second layer holds a total of twelve bodhisattvas, three to a side with the central image on each side larger and on a more elaborate throne than those flanking it. The top layer holds four Buddhas with their attendant bodhisattvas. The uppermost portion of this piece is not decorated and a slot has been cut into the top which would have held an image of Vairocana, the ultimate Buddha. Thus this stupa is a miniature representation of the Buddhist universe, beginning with the lowest forms (animals and sentient beings) at the bottom and finishing with the ultimate Buddha at the top.

This piece reveals both the strengths and weaknesses of ivory. The carver was able to create in great detail and in very small scale a complex and aesthetically pleasing work of art. However, the piece is cracked, rubbed, and much of the exposed detail has been lost to breakage and wear.

8. Throne leg
Indian, from Orissa, Mughal dynasty, 16th-17th century
H: 16″
Eugene Fuller Memorial Collection, 66.6

Orissa was a major center of ivory carving in the thirteenth century and through the Mughal period. Among the ivories produced at Orissa were a series of throne legs, the earliest surviving example dating from the thirteenth century. The piece illustrated here follows closely the form of these early throne legs but can be dated by style to the sixteenth or seventeenth century.

In the earlier ivories discussed above (nos. 6 and 7), ivory was used to create religious images; in the throne leg from Orissa, the association in India between ivory and wealth and power becomes apparent. Although no complete example has survived, it is likely that entire thrones for the royalty were created from this medium. All the surviving throne legs from Orissa are decorated with the same hybrid beast, the *gajavirala,* which has the head, front limbs, and certain body parts of an elephant, with the body and claws of a lion. The elephant and the lion are the two most powerful beasts in Indian symbolism: the lion is a solar symbol and represents royal authority, while the elephant represents the supports of the phenomenal world and royal power.

This throne leg is remarkably complex. The base is turned, with every indication of having been worked on a lathe. The lowest level of decoration on what must be considered the back of the leg holds two horsemen, their mounts stepping on a pig; above them are two birds, which flank the tail of the beast. Additional birds may be found behind each of the riders. The back of the animal is covered with a long curling mane and at the top of the decorated section is a marvelous crowned gargoyle with human arms and hands. At the base of the front of this leg is a female figure which must represent fertility, she stands between the massive rear legs of the beast which end in claws. This side of the leg is also decorated with a curling mane and belled harness, but ends in the head of a bejeweled elephant. A pair of claws emerges from beneath the elephant's trunk and grasps the side of the leg. The top of the leg is undecorated and cut into a four-sided tenon which must have fit into the base of the throne. The entire fantastic ensemble is carved with a great deal of attention to detail and finish typical of the arts of the Mughal period.

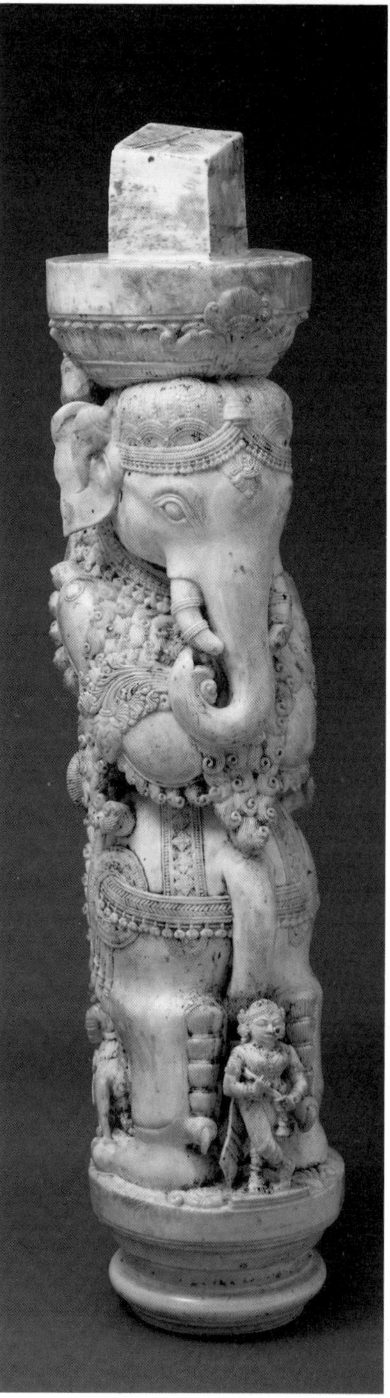

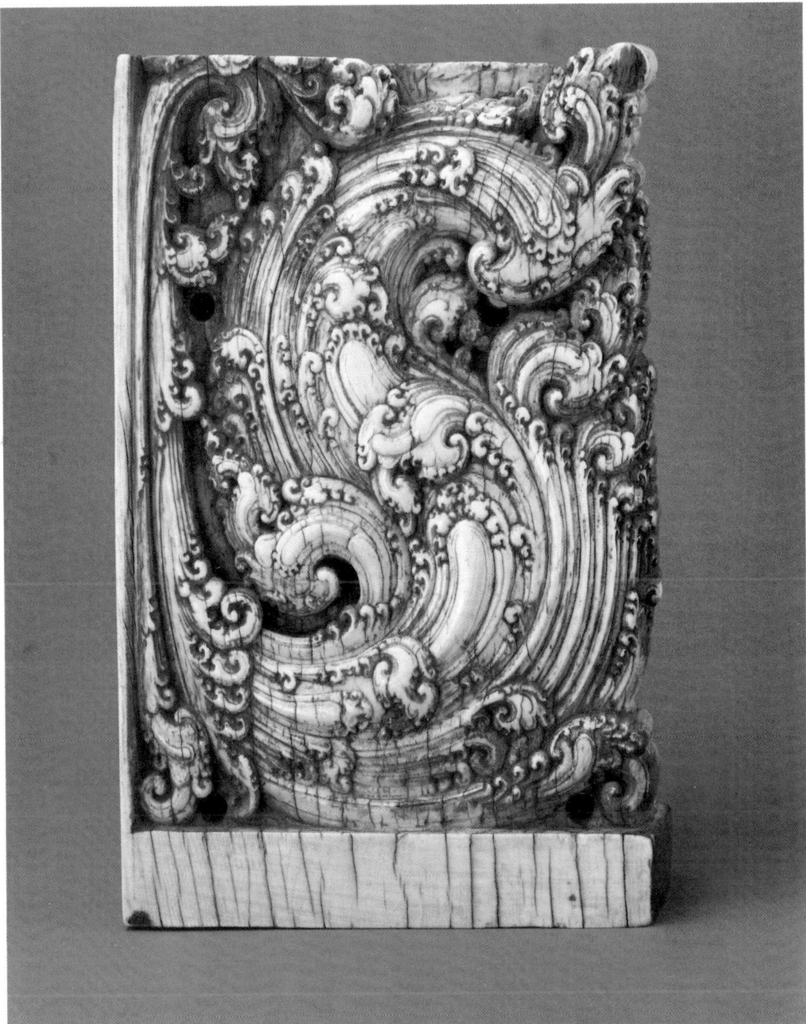

9. Section from ivory door jamb
Sri Lanka, from Kandy,
18th century
H: 6 ¼″; W: 4 ⅞″
Eugene Fuller Memorial Collection, 58.34

The ruling families of Sri Lanka trace their origins back to Brahman Aryan people who invaded the island from Northern India. However, when Buddhism was introduced in the fourth century B.C., it was adopted as the primary religion and remained so throughout most of the history of this island nation. Unlike in continental India, Hinduism did not supplant Buddhism in Sri Lanka and this led to major differences in art and culture. In ivory carving this difference was significant: Hindu prohibitions against the killing of animals limited work in ivory in much of India; Buddhism does not have such prohibitions, and this craft was practiced extensively in Sri Lanka.

By the late eighteenth century Sri Lanka had already suffered from the presence of the Portuguese and the Dutch; the last remaining outpost of independent Sri Lankan culture was held by the people who dwelled in the highlands of the island with their capital at Kandy. During the early part of the nineteenth century, the island was invaded by the British, and the last of the independent rulers fell in 1815. From that point on, Sri Lanka changed from a self-sufficient nation to one reliant on trade and foreign goods and much of what was unique to the culture of this island was lost.

This carving was once part of what must have been an exceedingly beautiful door jamb that probably belonged to a major temple in the city of Kandy. It was created in the eighteenth century during the last flowering of Sri Lankan culture. It is decorated with the *liya pata,* one of the most characteristic motifs of the arts of Sri Lanka. Among other decorative uses, it is found in wood, ivory, and other material as architectural detailing, quite frequently in door jambs similar to this example. This motif is apparently based on some type of leaf; over long periods of evolution it has become very elaborate with flame or wavelike curling linear patterns which often end in volutes and flourishes. This piece is elaborately carved on the front; the back is roughly finished with a slot carved along one edge and four holes drilled for mounting.

Japan

10. Netsuke
Cicada and pine branch
Kanayama Ungai, 19th century
Japanese, Edo period, dated 1866
Boar's tusk and black horn
H: 3⅜″
Duncan MacTavish Fuller Memorial Collection, 33.531

Reclining deer
Okatomo (before 1781)
Japanese, Edo period, 18th century
H: 1¼″
Duncan MacTavish Fuller Memorial Collection, 33.464

Ginko leaf
Kaigyokusai (1813-92)
Japanese, Edo period, 19th century
H: ⅝″
Duncan MacTavish Fuller Memorial Collection, 35.64

Infant's doll *(amagatsu)* Masanao (before 1781)
Japanese, Edo period, 18th century
H: 1¼″
Duncan MacTavish Fuller Memorial Collection, 33.549

Buddhist lion (Shishi) on rock with rattling ball
Japanese, Edo period, early 19th century
H: 1½″
Duncan MacTavish Fuller Memorial Collection, 33.450

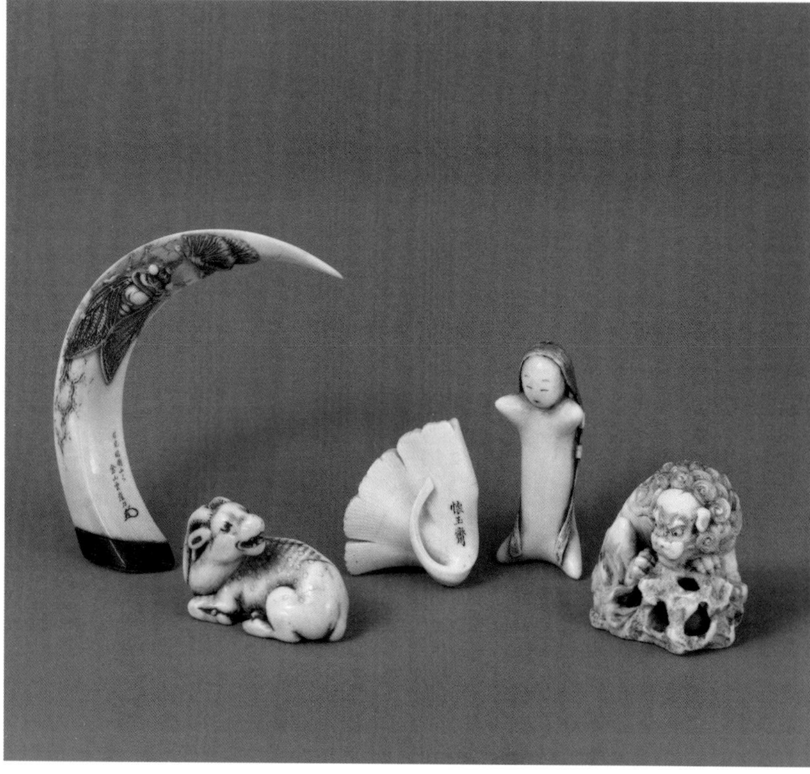

Perhaps the major use of ivory in Japan, and certainly the form most frequently seen in the West, is in the small and often elaborately carved toggles known as netsuke. The original purpose of these toggles was to suspend objects such as small containers *(inro)* from the belt (obi); as the tradition developed, many were made for purely decorative purposes. The carving of netsuke filled a gap in the three-dimensional arts of Japan. With the decline of Buddhist sculpture following the Kamakura period, the sculptural tradition in Japan lost its main form of expression. Netsuke became one of the major, albeit miniature, forms of sculpture in later Japanese art; many of the earliest netsuke retain themes and styles seen in Buddhist arts. As this art developed, themes expanded to include almost every aspect of Japanese life and belief. The group illustrated here, which includes plants, animals, and humans, represents only a fraction of this range.

Netsuke are carved from a variety of media, but ivory is one of the most popular since it allows carving in very fine detail and in very small scale, qualities that are an absolute necessity for an art form that rarely exceeds two inches in its largest dimension. The elephant is not native to Japan and all ivory was imported or came from other sources, such as the fine carving of a netsuke from boar tusk illustrated here. Because of their small scale, ivory netsuke were often carved from material remaining from other uses, the most frequently mentioned are the wedge-shaped pieces left over from making plectum guards and plucks for a popular stringed instrument known as the shamisen.

By the middle of the Edo period, netsuke had become very popular, and the more prominent craftsmen creating them were able to demand the highest quality materials, including the finest ivory. Many pieces from this period and later are signed. Signed pieces among the netsuke illustrated here include the child's doll, signed Masanao, an artist from Kyoto active in the eighteenth century; the cicada and pine, signed by Kanaya Ungai and dated 1866; the reclining stag, signed by Okatomo, another Kyoto artist active during the eighteenth century; and the ginko leaf, signed by Kaigyokusai Masatsugu, an artist active in Osaka during the nineteenth century. The carving of these netsuke, which ranges from the refined elegance of the child's doll to the intricate detail of the Buddhist lion, reveals the diversity Japanese craftsmen achieved in a medium as flexible as ivory.

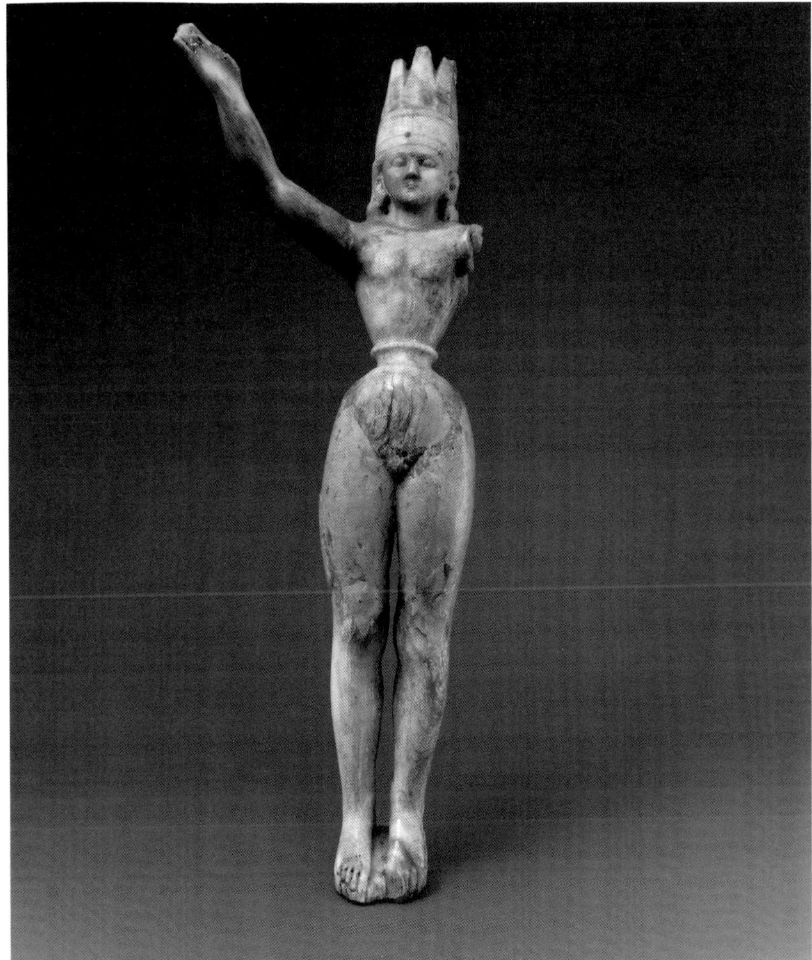

Ancient Mediterranean

11. Boy-god (Bull-leaper)
Minoan, c. 1600 B.C.
H: 6 ⅞″
Margaret E. Fuller Fund, 57.56

This rare example of Minoan ivory sculpture, a boy-god, has survived nearly 3,500 years of geologic and historic upheaval in the Aegean as testimony to the rich tradition of Minoan ivory figurines and reliefs in ancient Crete. Small-scale ivory figures of acrobats from the Minoan bull rituals found at Knossos and an ivory and gold snake goddess in the collection of the Museum of Fine Arts, Boston, all dated circa 1600 B.C., share the boy-god's lifelike tension, characteristic of Minoan ivory sculpture. The boy-god and the Boston snake goddess have been attributed by Sir Arthur Evans, the British excavator of the Palace of Minos early in this century, to the ivory treasury of the Palace of Minos at Knossos. The boy-god, so-named by Sir Arthur, was originally part of the archaeologist's personal collection, although not excavated by him; it had appeared without provenance on the art market in Paris after World War I.

The boy-god wears a three-pointed headdress and constricting circle belt which may have been covered with gold. His wedge-shaped torso and narrow waist are typical of the illustrations of young athletes in the lively frescoes of the Minoan palaces. His arms are raised in a solemn gesture, the left arm unfortunately lost at the shoulder where it had been joined by an ivory peg, typical of Minoan work. The head of the youth is tilted back, his long hair falling on his shoulders, his body in an uplifted arc with toes carrying his weight on the wedgelike platform under his feet. His pose is certainly suggestive of a bull-leaper's "salute" before vaulting over the horns of a bull in the Minoan ritualistic game so often portrayed in other art forms. A small peg extends from the base of the figure indicating that the sculpture would have been inserted into a platform or other object for display, probably with other figures.

The ivory is discolored from age and from old wax restorations on the thighs. Small pinholes on the band above the forehead and in the area of the groin may suggest the attachment points for gold foil decoration. The youth probably wore the distinctive Minoan loincloth fabricated in gold. The Boston snake goddess has gold bands encircling her flounced skirt attached by gold pins, and holds two gold snakes.

Medieval Europe

12. Mirror back: Siege of the Castle of Love

French, Ile-de-France School, Paris, c. 1320-50
H: 4 ½″; W: 4 ¼″
Donald E. Frederick Memorial Collection, 49.37

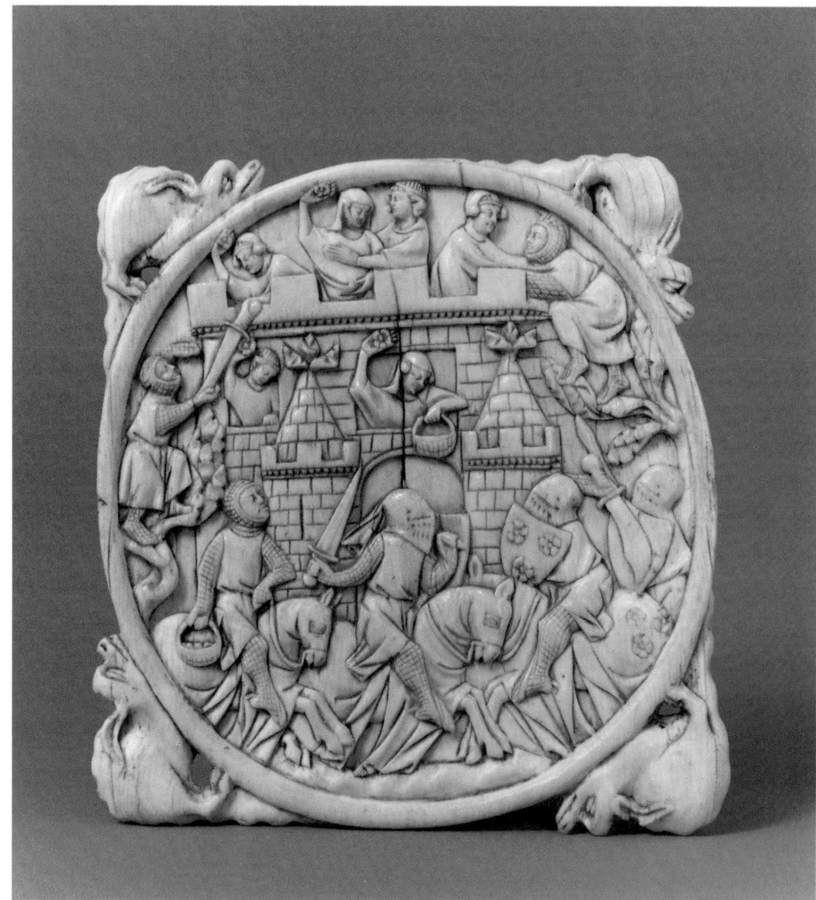

This fourteenth-century mirror back, depicting the *Siege of the Castle of Love,* is one of the finest examples known of its kind. The typical Gothic mirror format of a circular field within squared corners formed by crouching wyverns, or fantastic beasts, encloses a masterful composition of the allegorical siege, a popular theme that appears in many variations on fourteenth-century secular objects.

At the center of this composition is a twin-turreted castle armed by noble ladies who are pelting their attackers, an army of knights in armor, with roses. Only the three jousting knights in the bottom register of the composition appear to be locked in actual combat. However, the emblem of roses on the shield and horse-trapping of the knight at right of this group, connects him with the overall romantic theme. The rest of the knights are eagerly climbing the walls of the castle, handing up their swords and being assisted by the "defenders" over the ramparts. The knight on horseback at lower left brings fresh ammunition in the form of a basket of roses. A knight who has reached the top of the parapet at center has already removed his chain mail and embraces a woman hurling her final rose of resistance. This male figure may suggest the god of love, sometimes seen at the apex of other siege compositions.

The subtle composition of compacted figures rotating around the hub of the castle gate reveals the virtuosity of this anonymous Gothic carver. Orderly harmony of form is achieved with maximum dynamic detail within the challenging confines of a circle. The hands of the two women at upper left actually overlap the rim of the mirror back in a note of assymetry, drawing attention to the amusing depiction of gentle *wyverns* napping on the rim, oblivious to the amorous turmoil within the circle.

The *Siege of the Castle of Love* was an allegory of the conquest of courtly love stemming from romance traditions of the late Middle Ages. The theme does not come from the well-known medieval chivalric poem "Romance of the Rose" as previously thought, but from an oral tradition of unknown origin that found its way to France, Germany, England, and Italy. Enactments of the castle of love's floral siege, with ladies portraying a symbolic resistance in the battle for their hearts, occurred during medieval festivals from the thirteenth century on.

The theme appears not only on ivory mirror backs and caskets, but in manuscripts, enamels, metalwork, and tapestries of the late medieval period. Its popularity relates to the prevalence of such themes of courtly love recorded in the literature, poetry, and songs of the period—an ideal of love played out within the code of chivalric honor.

The museum's ivory mirror back would have held a polished metal mirror made of speculum, an alloy of copper and tin. Some mirrors were enclosed in paired ivory covers, which would have held the mirror upright on their squared edges when open. Fourteenth-century manuscript paintings show women using ivory combs and mirrors, some attached to the woman's belt by a fine chain. The images carved on the ivory mirror case would have evoked romantic fantasy for the noblewoman as she contemplated her own image.

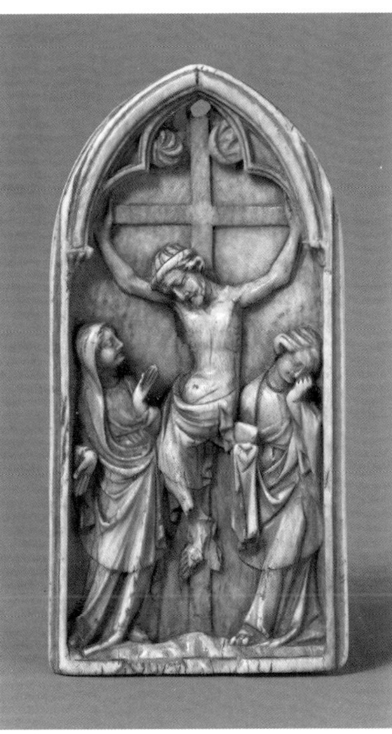

13. Pax: Crucifixion
French, 1350-1400
H: 4 ¼″; W: 2⅛″
Gift of Dorothy Chatterton Malone in memory of her father, Reverend Herbert I. Chatterton, 50.106

Ivory was regarded as an important precious material for objects used in service of the medieval church. Its intrinsic value as an exotic imported commodity was augmented by biblical reference and historical associations with the early Christian church. There are many references in the Bible, including the description of King Solomon's ivory throne overlaid with gold (I Kings 10:18), and several poetic references in the Song of Solomon. Early Christian ivories, which included Roman ivories converted to Christian use, survived as venerated objects in the church treasuries of Western Europe. Roman consular diptychs, ivory writing tablets made to commemorate the appointment of consuls ruling the Empire, were adapted as ecclesiastical diptychs which were inscribed with names of those to be remembered during the celebration of the Mass.

Ivory circular boxes, pyxides, made from a tusk cross-section, were often used in the medieval church to hold the sanctified bread for Communion. These pyxides were modeled on ivory boxes used by wealthy Roman women to hold jewels. Ivory panels combined with gold, silver, and gems served as book covers for liturgical manuscripts and as panels on reliquaries. Bishops' croziers were often made of ivory, as were liturgical combs used during holy rituals such as baptism and investiture of priests. Large sections of elephant tusk have been preserved in carved vessels such as the situla, or holy-water bucket, and the oliphant (corruption of the word "elephant"), a ritual horn. Three-dimensional ivory figures of Christ and the Virgin Mary were also carved during the Gothic period.

The pax (meaning "peace") was a new liturgical object introduced in the Middle Ages. In the Gothic period the pax was used as an icon to transmit the ritual kiss from the priest to his assistants to the congregation before the sacrifice of Communion on the altar. The museum's pax has a shallow slot carved in the back which would have accommodated a handle that was used to present the icon during the kiss-of-peace ritual.

The imagery of the Crucifixion on the pax is appropriate to its use preceding the sacrifice of Christ's body and blood embodied in the bread and wine of Communion. The Gothic-style figures communicate a gentle pathos—the Virgin Mary and Saint John mourning in restrained gestures that lead the eye to the figure of the dead Christ. Christ's arms form an uplifting gesture, even while nailed to the cross, alluding to the triumph of the Resurrection.

With great skill and economy of form the carver has enclosed the sensitively portrayed group within a Gothic pointed trefoil arch. The reverse arch of Christ's extended arms serves to complete the lobes of the Gothic trefoil—a reminder of the Holy Trinity—while His body forms a symbolic supporting column. Calligraphic representations of the sun and moon are tucked under the edges of the arch, symbolizing the unnatural eclipse that darkened the earth during the Crucifixion, as described in Matthew 27:45. This representation, with the spiral sun on the left and crescent moon on the right of the cross, is traced to Gothic art from ninth-century Carolingian ivories.

14. Plaque: Conversion of St. Paul

Attributed to Dominicus Stainhart (1655-1712) and Franz Stainhart I (1651-1695)
German, late 17th century
H: 6 ¾″; L: 12 ⅜″
Margaret E. Fuller Purchase Fund, 58.38

This masterful baroque plaque is an outstanding example of the tremendous output of German ivory carving in the seventeenth and eighteenth centuries. Ivory carvers from southern Germany enjoyed the greatest renown, including several families of artists such as the Stainhart brothers to whom the museum's plaque is attributed. Dominicus and Franz Stainhart spent nine years in Italy as young artists, including six in Rome, immersing themselves in the Italian baroque style. Like many German ivory sculptors, they carved a variety of precious materials such as coral, amber, and mother-of-pearl, with woodcarving as a companion skill. The brothers were known for their ivory bas-relief plaques, represented by examples in both Rome and Munich.

Decorative plaques, such as this *Conversion of St. Paul,* became an important ivory form as the new luxury material of porcelain began to eclipse ivory's popularity as the medium for small-scale figurative sculpture. Large ivory plaques were made possible by new technical advances: the ivory sheet could now be pared from the circumference of the tusk, softened with a solution of phosphoric acid, and flattened under pressure to achieve a plaque considerably wider than the normal five- to six-inch cross-section of a large African tusk.

The religious subject matter of this plaque suggests that it may have decorated the furnishings of a baroque church or may have been an object of private contemplation. Images of saints were popular in the art of the Counter-Reformation, and the dramatic story of St. Paul's conversion to Christianity lent itself well to the theatrical tastes of the baroque.

As described in the Acts of the Apostles (Acts 9:1-9), Paul was struck by a blinding light while on the road to Damascus as a Roman soldier on a mission to deliver Christians to Jerusalem for persecution. Paul fell to the earth, blinded, hearing the voice of Jesus Christ saying "... why persecutest thou me?" The men around him "stood speechless, hearing a voice, but seeing no man."

The drama on the plaque is depicted at the moment of Paul's bewildered query as "he trembling and astonished said, 'Lord, what wilt thou have me to do?'." Paul lies on his back, where he has fallen from his startled horse, staring with unseeing eyes at the heavens above. His companions react to the shock of the event: one supporting Paul as he gestures toward the voice of Christ, one attempting to control his rearing mount on the left, and one retrieving Paul's fleeing horse, which is turning its head in terror toward the apparition of Christ.

The Stainharts used the technique of bas-relief carving to achieve a superb sense of light and dark, depth, and dynamic action. The horse on the left rears out of the plaque as naturally as if emerging from a liquid medium. The head and shield of his rider extend into space as sculptural objects, casting deep shadows on the face of the plaque that successfully suggest the brilliance of light radiating from the image of Christ at upper right. The deep sculptural rendering of Paul's reclining body leads smoothly into the low relief of his left leg and the sketch of his horse racing into the distance, with distance implied by the shallowness of carving.

The typical baroque use of swirling action is underscored by billowing draperies that bind the three figures of the foreground composition together. The clouds around Christ turn and boil, the men's hair and the horses' manes stream in a rush of movement. The viewer's eye centers on the tension of shock in Paul's face, as directed by the gaze of his two companions and rearing horse at left. The eye then lifts along the beseeching arm of Paul to the spiritual center of the composition, the apparition of Christ holding the orb of the Christian church as he instigates the drama below, invisible to its players.

19

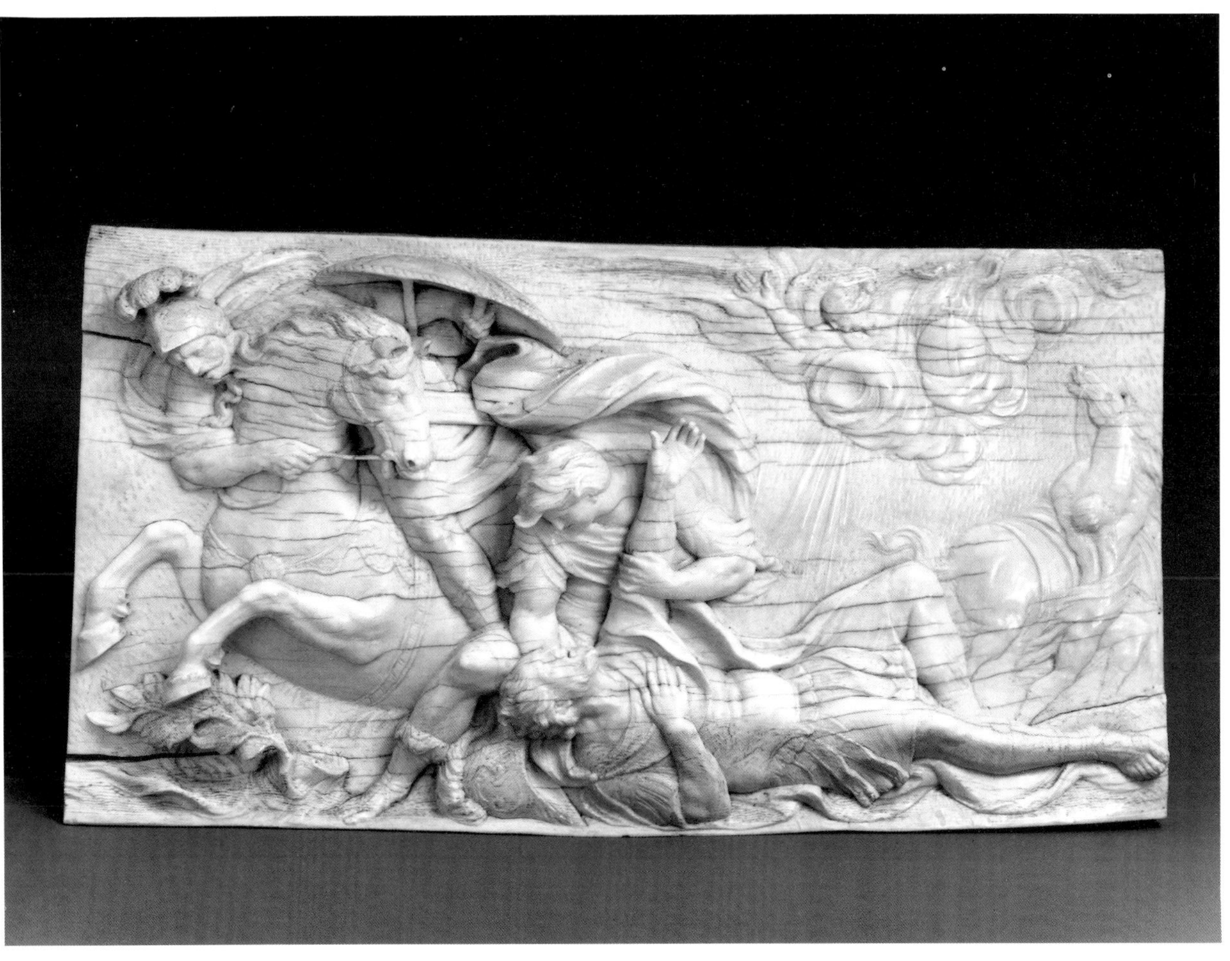

Africa

15. Salt cellar with seated figure and crocodiles
African, Sierra Leone, "Afro-Portuguese" style, late 15th-mid-16th century
H: 8⅛″
Gift of Nasli and Alice Heeramaneck, 68.31

Salt cellar with four seated figures
African, Sierra Leone, "Afro-Portuguese" style, late 15th-mid-16th century
H: 12⅛″
Katherine White Collection, 81.17.189

A unique chapter in ivory history and African-European relations is commemorated in these cellars. They originate from an era of discovery when African artists and European explorers were encountering each other for the first time and creative sparks were ignited. Less than one hundred of these "curiosities" are thought to have survived intact from that time, and the museum is fortunate to have two prime examples.

Europeans had long coveted ivory as a rare commodity. Prior to the fifteenth century, it was supplied through the costly channels of Asian and Egyptian merchants. When in that century Europeans first sailed down the West African coast, they quickly satisfied their yearning for "white gold," finding vast quantities at very little cost. Seeking out raw resources was one aspect of this initial contact; the other was the momentous step of opening up the unknown "dark continent." As the first tourists to reach West African shores, European navigators sought souvenirs to carry home.

Simultaneously, Africans were watching white Europeans emerge from caravels. Their interactions with these explorers were subtly registered in hybrid art forms like cellars for salt carved on commission. Carvers had fashioned ivory implements before, but the pedestal cup being requested posed new challenges. The form had been devised by European silver- and goldsmiths as a showcase for their technical skill and imagination. Renaissance cellars were covered in layers of profuse and extravagant detailing. Africans were equally inventive in their response to the metal cellar form and created tour de force ivory renditions.

These cellars follow the ornamental vocabulary of European metal examples to a surprising extent. Curving pedestals, bulbous knops, as well as minute granulation and incised borders are all replicated in ivory. Both these examples display a global center with bands that might imitate the European model of coconut cups and ostrich eggs mounted in metal strapwork. Slender crocodiles crawl over the surface of a cellar, with a gaunt bearded man seated on a tripod throne. A lacy open-worked base is created on the other cellar with alternating men and women wearing striped pantaloons, skirts, and peaked caps. The heads at the tops of these cellars help identify the origin of the artists who carved them as Bullom/Temne, where stone carvings with the same facial features are carved. Three hundred years of no written documentation makes iconographic interpretation difficult. Indeed, for two centuries the cellars were thought to be Indian, Turkish, or European in origin. Only in recent decades have Portuguese customs records confirmed their African creation.

In the fifteenth and sixteenth centuries, such salt cellars became an integral part of a Renaissance dining table. Positioned near the "master's seat," they accented his careful dispensation of salt, then a precious spice, to guests. In this context, a cellar depicting Africana would have been a conversation piece promoting discussion about the newly explored continent. This juxtaposition of European form with African style lasted for less than a century. First contacted in 1462, Sierra Leonians were soon beseiged by inland invasions that caused a halt in carving. European trade also ceased its patronage. When it became apparent what huge quantities of unworked ivory were available, merchants scanned the coast to collect hundreds and thousands of tusks yearly. The raw material, rather than carvings, became a source of fast fortunes.

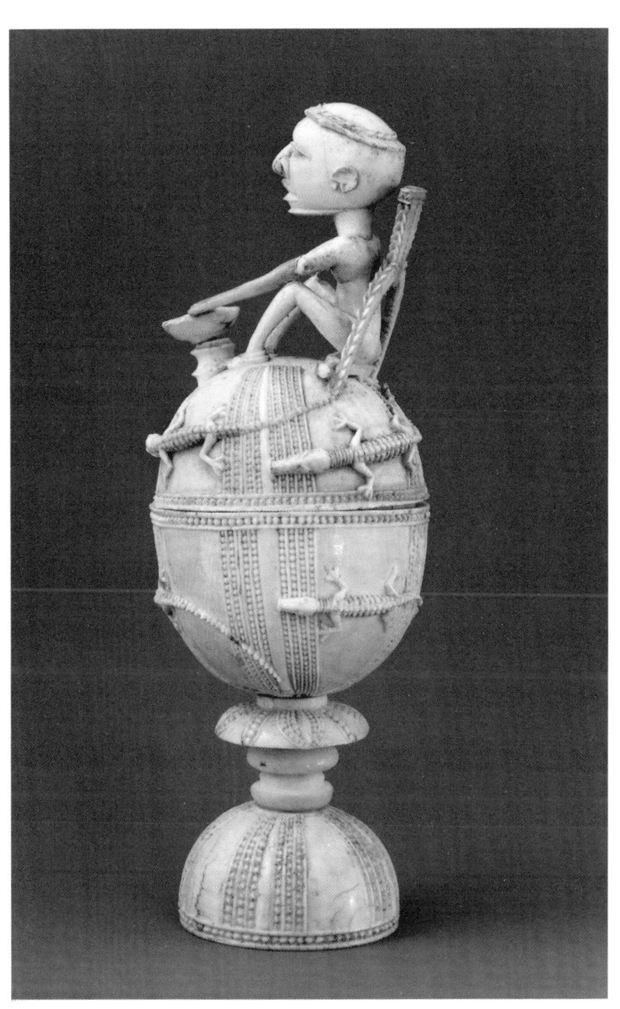

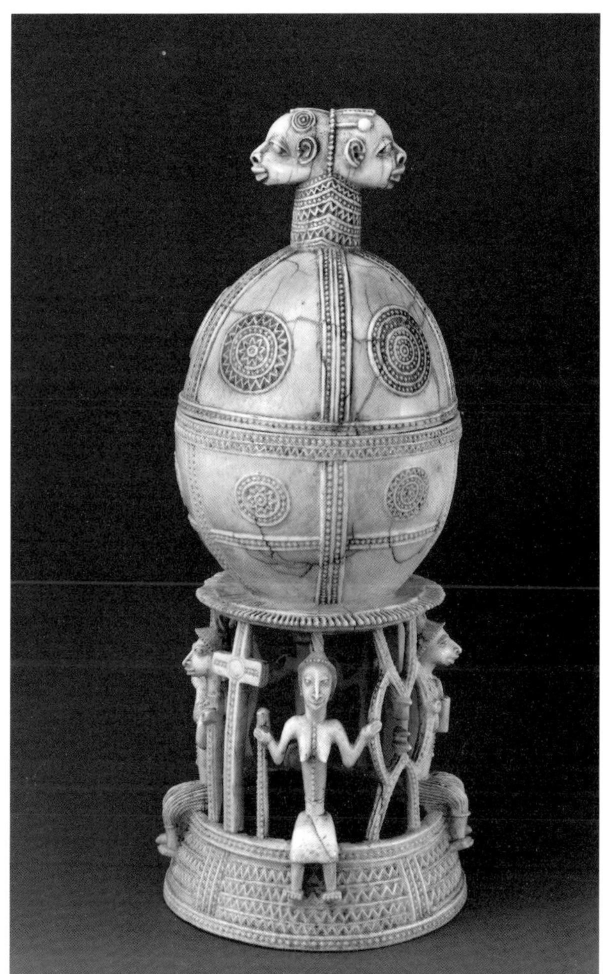

16. Mother and child
African, Nigeria, Yoruba, Owo
H: 5 ⅞″
Katherine White Collection, 81.17.605

Equestrian
African, Nigeria, Yoruba
H: 4⅛″
Gift of Nasli and Alice Heeramaneck, 68.27

Ivory lends itself to miniaturization, as is demonstrated in these two carvings from Nigeria. Both can be held in the palm of a hand, but neither spares any detail or sculptural strength. Each depicts a prevalent theme in African art: the mother and child, and the equestrian.

No part of the mother's anatomy is left undecorated. She has tatoos on her chest, and wears bracelets and necklaces, beads, and a lip plug. Tatoos are made by traveling specialists who cut small incisions and rub soot into them to cause black designs to emerge in shallow relief on the skin. Textured patterns continue in her elaborate braided hairstyle, serrated eyebrows, and layers of jewelry.

Motherhood has a distinctive status among the Yoruba. A woman nursing her child with full breasts is considered ritually pure. For two or three years she feeds her baby, is sexually abstinent, and is filled with a generous dedication to the overseeing of life. In this state of sanctity, such women are deemed most appropriate to carry out acts of worship for Yoruba deities. Rather than simply conveying fertility, such figures also represent the spiritual vitality of motherhood. This mother is carved in a style now known as that of Owo, a town on the outskirts of Yorubaland and close to the Benin kingdom. As a carving center, it is becoming recognized as an entrepot where an ivory export industry may once have flourished.

Men on horseback also connote a position of privilege in Yorubaland. This man may represent a hunter/warrior who is given the horse to ride on royal business. Given the difficulty of breeding and sustaining horses in tropical Africa, riders were either cavalrymen or persons authorized to carry out auspicious duties. This rider carries no weapons, but is protected nonetheless. A tuft of hair extends from the crown of his head, and is likely to cover incisions that were made to receive medicinal preparations rubbed into his scalp to render him intrepid during battle. Historic accounts of the cavalry warfare conducted by the Yoruba lead to an understanding of a form of war that might not require many weapons. Instead, actual combat was rare, while psychological intimidation and sieges of towns were more readily practiced. Nineteenth-century accounts record the puzzlement of the British that Yoruba warriors used nine-tenths of their ammunition for salutes and only one-tenth in combat. One Yoruba scholar has explained that this reticence to use deadly weapons stems from a belief that it is better to live for a cause than to die for one and cites the following: *"Eri t'o ku tire l'o gbe"* (Whoever dies, it's his fortune that is terminated).

It is not known how either of these ivories was used, or exactly how old they are. Since ivory ownership was restricted, they were likely part of the paraphernalia of the *babalawo* or priest of divination. Stored with the sacred palm nuts used to cast determinations of clients' destinies, they would contribute to the process of interpreting fate.

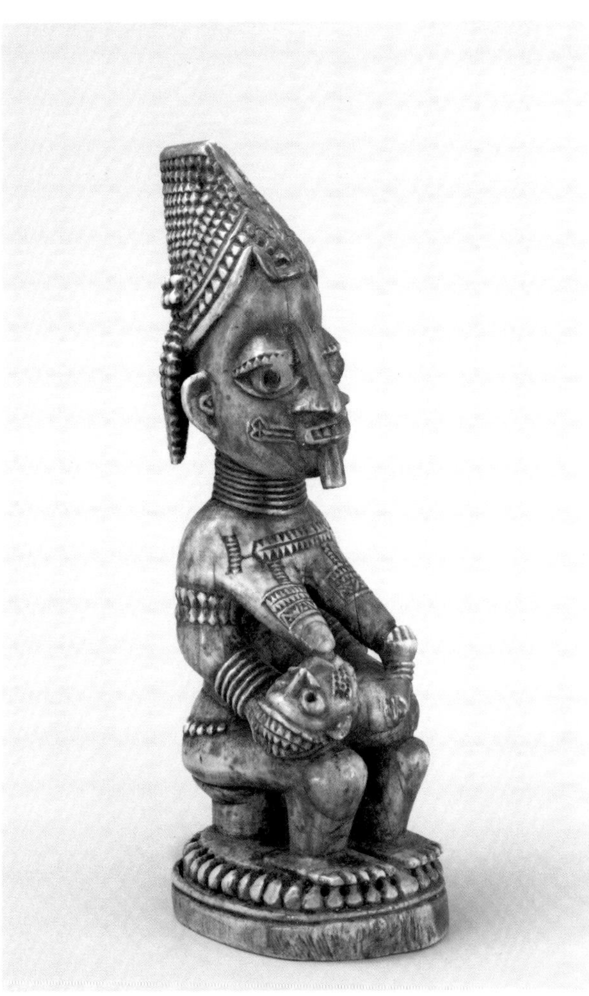

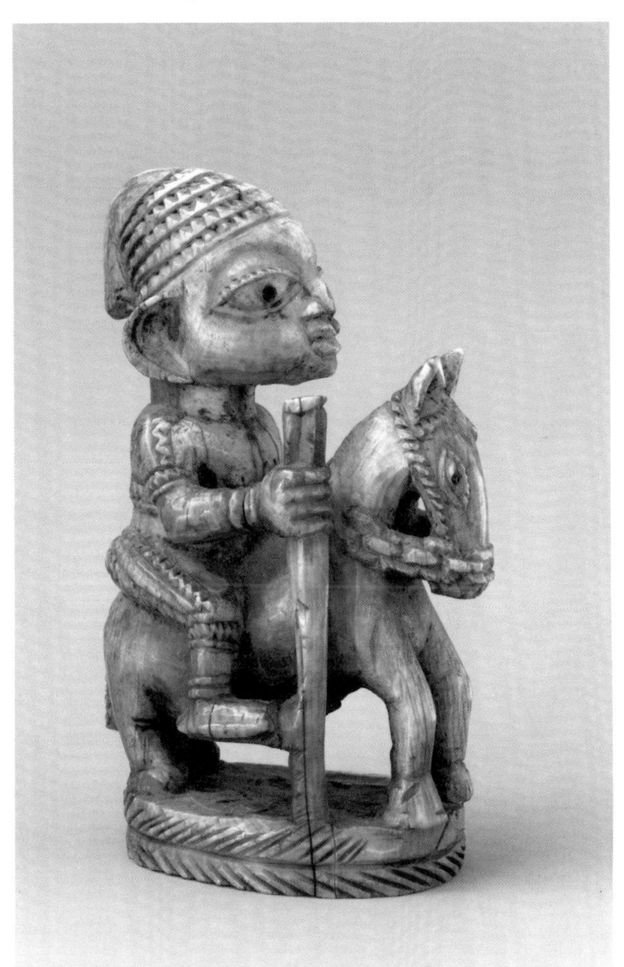

17. Cane top with figure and chicken
African, Ivory Coast, Akye
H: 6 ¼″
Gift of Nasli and Alice Heeramaneck, 68.29

Prim and properly seated, this gentleman has previously been typecast as the image of a European soldier stationed at a post on the African coast. Recent research leads to a different identity—that of an African leader who has adopted imported dress and implements to support an elevated position in Akye society.

This figure comes from a region that earned the name of "Ivory Coast" in the seventeenth and eighteenth centuries when large quantities of ivories were extracted during trade with European merchants. While the region supplied ivory tusks, not much Akye ivory sculpture has survived.

Seven carved, elongated pommels like this are now in collections. All are thought to have served as tops to canes carried by Akye leaders. Since the Akye do not rely on inherited positions, they choose their leaders with care. One criterion for ascendancy used to be that the candidate have enough wealth to display staffs, stools, ivory trumpets, and gold jewelry to demonstrate his wealth and rank. Similarly, European imports like brimmed hats, buttoned jackets, a flintlock rifle, and a high-backed chair would suggest a man of superior resources. The capacity of ivory to illustrate detail is fully exploited in this depiction of the man's pipecurled sidelocks, buttons, eyes, and incised figuration or lettering.

As if to disrupt the decorum of the tidy gentleman beneath, a grinning rooster perches atop his hat. Whether the rooster is meant to be as mischievous as his animated face makes him out to be is not known.

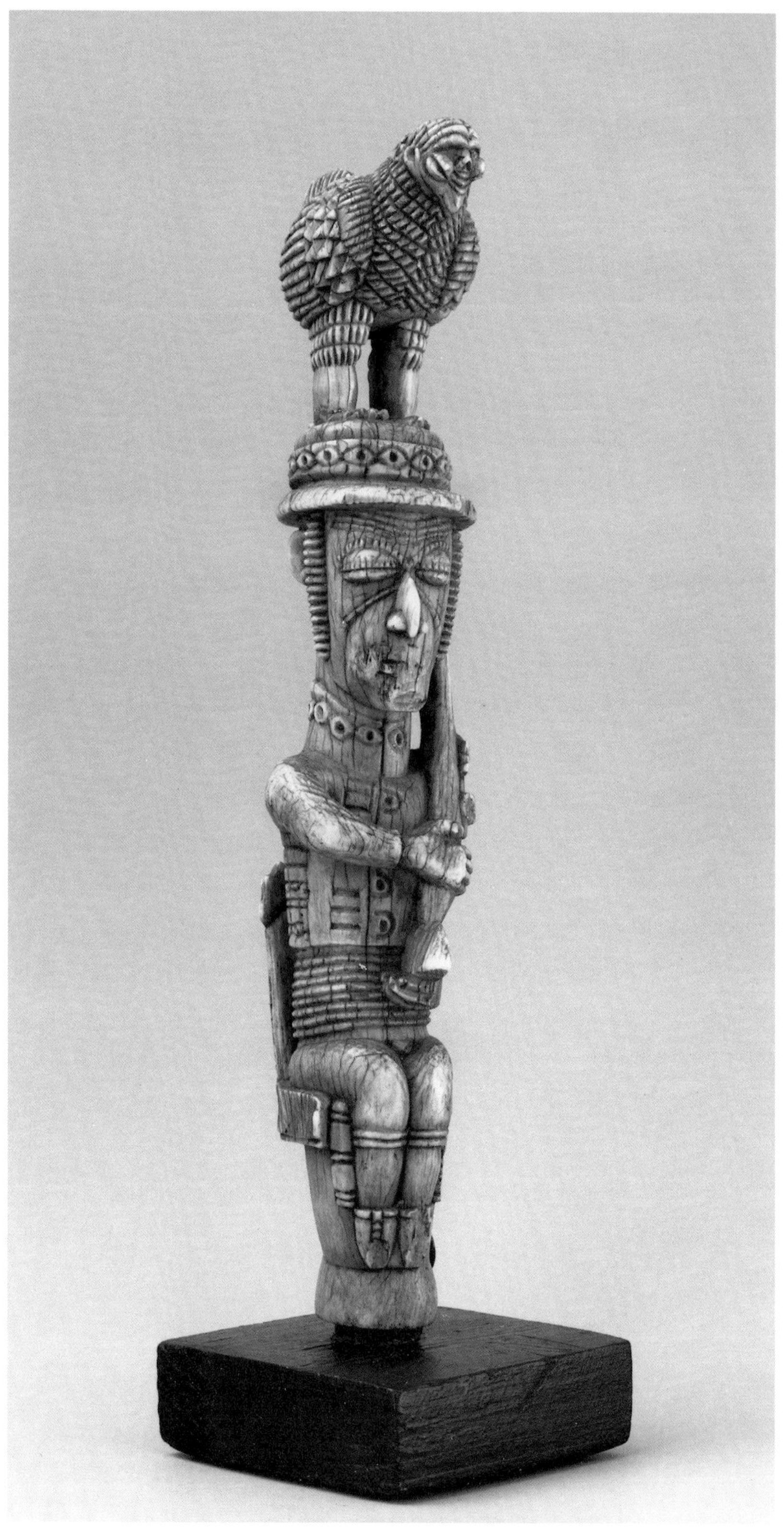

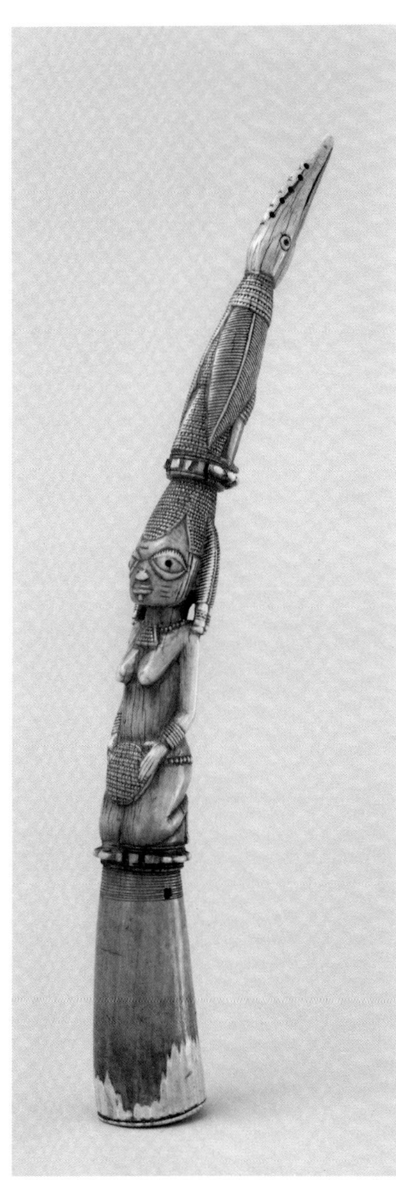

According to Yoruba belief, each person's soul kneels at birth before the Sky God to choose a destiny. If this request is made humbly and deemed reasonable, one's character, occupation, and success will be established for life. Yet, this destiny may be muted by the chaos and disorder that also reign in the world. When one becomes confused by misfortune and despair, one kneels again in the presence of a *babalawo* or diviner-priest.

To begin this consultation, the *babalawo* recites a series of invocations to the gods and ancestors. Next, he takes a tapper with the calm image of a woman and a bird, rattles the clapper within, and taps a tray for divination. In doing so, he calls Orunmila to be present and watch over the proceedings. Orunmila is the special deity who knows what destiny was chosen by all clients and who knows the hidden possibilities in one's life; he even knows how to activate *ashe,* the power to make things happen. In the further steps of this Ifa process, priests recite verses from the corpus of oral poetry to aid the client in determining what changes or sacrifices are necessary for overcoming obstacles and clarifying his or her destiny.

Thus, this woman and bird have probably witnessed the turning of fate for many Yoruba suppliants. Her nudity and her pose serve as a reminder of the sacred circumstance under which one knelt to receive one's personal future. Rich textures interrupt the smoothness of her skin, as her plaited hair, an Islamic tirah necklace, a fan, and beads adorn her body. Both the woman and the bird have been skillfully blended into the curvature of the tip of a tusk. The bird is called the *eyele* or "bird of the home." It was known in myth as a bird unable to have children until a diviner determined that a sacrifice was needed to create a male and female for the species; then, of course, birth took place.

Ivory is a medium reserved among the Yoruba for the use of kings, certain elders, and *babalawos.* An esteemed *babalawo* may accumulate a distinguished set of artworks to underline his effectiveness. His ability to interpret the laws of fate and to help men and women view their problems within the confusing world at large is a skill admired by clients, who may present him with artworks for his profession. This example has acquired a caramel color after years of handling and baths in palm oil, signifying that it served as an inspiration to its owner.

18. Divination tapper (Iroke Ifa)
African, Nigeria, Eastern Yoruba
H: 15 ½″
Gift of Nasli and Alice Heeramaneck, 68.26

19. Lidded container
African, Nigeria, Benin Kingdom, late 18th-19th century
H: 3 ½″
Katherine White Collection, 81.17.499

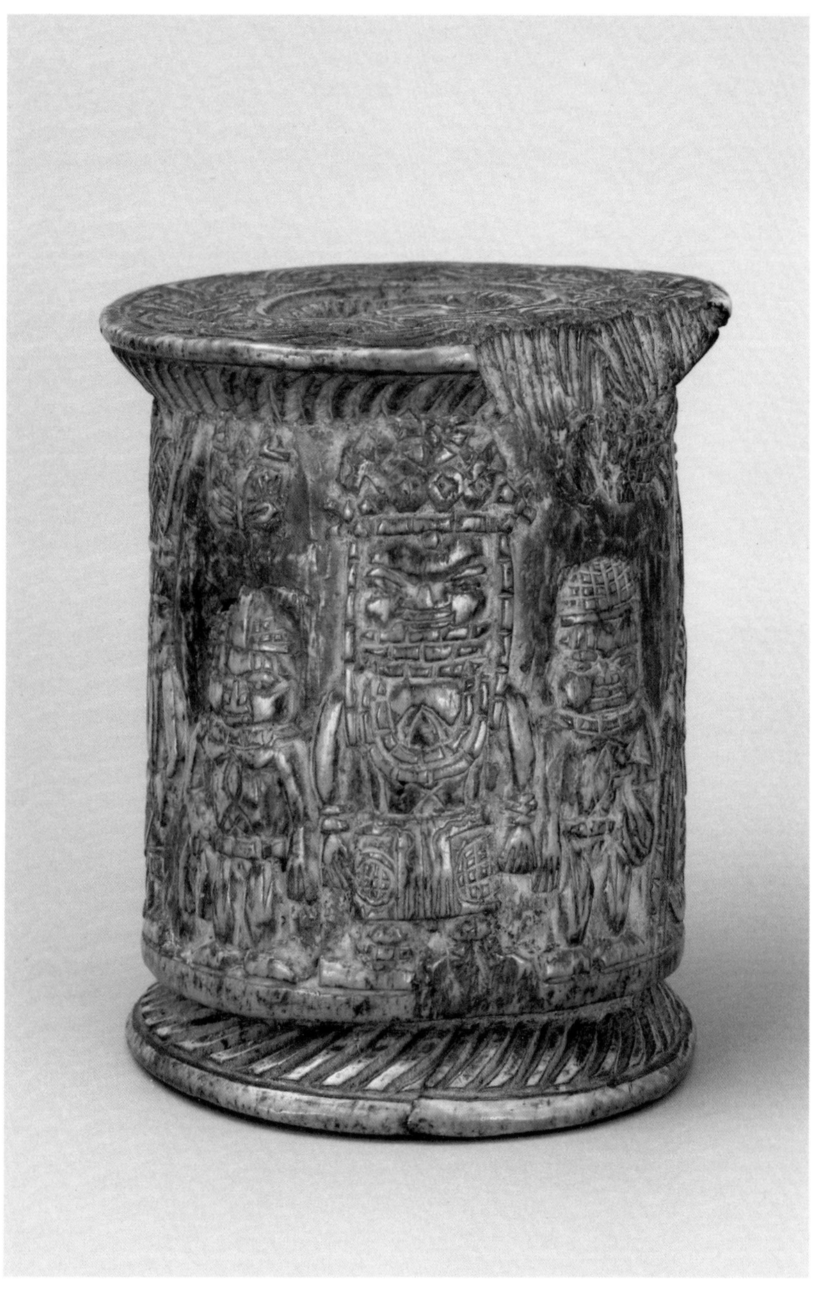

Despite its miniature size, this container is a detailed historical document of an African kingdom renowned for its ivory artistry. From the earliest traces of the Benin hegemony in the thirteenth century to the contemporary court, ivory has been a guarded medium in Benin culture. All hunting, trade, and important carving of ivory once came under the control of the Benin's divine king, the Oba. Only he gave permission to hunt elephants; he automatically owned the first tusk to touch the ground of any dying elephant and could purchase the other if he so chose. In centuries past, the Oba's palace courtyard stockpiled thousands of tusks for bargaining with foreign traders. A guild of carvers was assigned the task of carving ivory ornaments for the exclusive use of royalty, and they were required to remain within the palace grounds while doing so.

Both practical and metaphorical reasons bolstered ivory's status among the Benin. Being more durable than wood and relatively permanent, it was deemed suitable for carrying scenes and symbols that were meant to be passed on to new generations. Ritually, white was a color denoting purity and sacred significance. As the reminder of the ponderous and long-lived elephant, ivory was also equated with the longevity of the succession of Benin kings.

The container itself can be interpreted as a capsule account of a visit to the court of one of Benin's outstanding kings, Oba Esigie, who forged trade and diplomatic associations with Portuguese mercenaries and missionaries in the sixteenth century. The sides of this cup illustrate a mixture of African and European personalities and symbols initiated during Esigie's reign.

At the far right of the roll-out relief, a man holds a spool-shaped box *(ekpokin)* over his head. Such boxes were made of wood, bark, and leopard skin and telescoped out to hold gifts and implements for the Oba's use. This ivory container is, in fact, a small version of such a cylindrical box and once held special beads or gifts for the Oba.

The Oba himself is shown with a female attendant at either side and two male officials flanking them. Garments composed of rectangular strands connote the distinctive red coral bead regalia worn by Benin royalty during public ceremonies. Accordingly, the Oba is encased in a coral crown with strands descending to frame his face, a coral choker, and coral necklaces. He wears bracelets, anklets, and a decorated waist cloth. He is accompanied by two supporters who may have served to remind everyone of his dangerous and divine role as "the terrifying Oba with strange feet so full of life force that they are a threat to the fertility of the earth." One woman carries a penannular bronze ring or manilla, traded by Europeans as a form of currency. Above the women's heads float a leopard face and a fish tail. Leopards are thought to share ideal leadership traits with the Oba: they are both graceful and awesome, able to contain destructive force and to use it swiftly when necessary. The fish that most often appears as the leopard's counterpart is the mudfish, an emblem of watery realms—cool, peaceful, and robust enough to survive dry conditions by tightly closing its gill slits. The Benin king is balanced by the king of forests and the king of fish.

A bearded Portuguese with long hair and pointed shoes stands to the right, holding strands of beads in one hand and a sword in the other. The Portuguese were closely involved with the kingdom's affairs in the sixteenth century and supplied the Oba with manillas, beads, troops, and advisors in exchange for ivory, slaves, pepper, and other produce. They also assisted the Oba's military commanders, of which the figure on the left may be one. He wears a basketry crown with a feather plume and carries a palmate sword. Both the feather and sword are respected signs of age and chieftaincy. By holding the sword with the point turned upward, this chief indicates his salutations and loyalty to the Oba.

Through this small ivory with its condensed sampling of Benin iconography, an impression of the complex life of the court can be sustained. In Benin City, this piece would have been joined by hundreds of brass plaques and other artistry to form a permanent record of a remarkable kingdom.

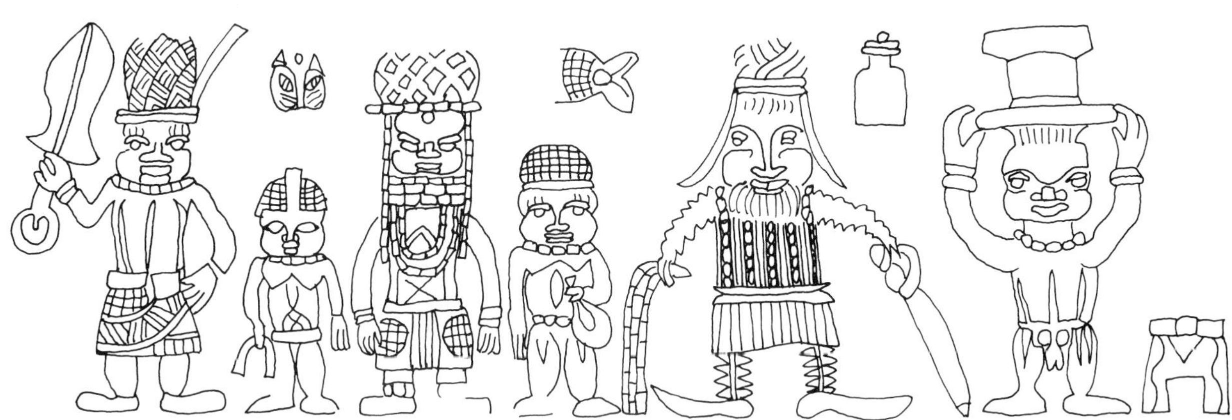

For Further Reading

Beigbeder, O. *Ivory.* New York: G. P. Putnam's Sons, 1965.

Blackmun, Barbara W. *Art as Statecraft: A King's Justification in Ivory; a carved tusk from Benin.* Geneva: Musee Barbier-Muller, 1984.

Burack, Benjamin. *Ivory and Its Uses.* Rutland, Vermont: Charles E. Tuttle Co., 1984.

Coomaraswamy, Dona Luisa. *The Arts and Crafts of India and Ceylon.* New York: Farrar, Straus and Co., 1964.

______. *Mediaeval Sinhalese Art.* 2nd edition. New York: Pantheon Books, Inc., 1956.

Davey, Neil K. *Netsuke: A comprehensive study based on the M. T. Hindson collection.* revised edition. New Jersey and London: Sotheby Publications, 1982.

Ezra, Kate. *African Ivories.* New York: The Metropolitan Museum of Art, 1984.

Maskell, Alfred. *Ivories.* Rutland, Vermont: Charles E. Tuttle Co., 1966.

Watson, William, ed. *Chinese Ivories from the Shang to the Qing.* London: Sotheby Publications, 1984.